MW00674980

ALEX & MADDIE

LIFE-SKILL LESSONS THROUGH ROLE-PLAY

Eight Units
Based On
Good
Character
Traits

WRITTEN BY
PAT VARGAS

ALEX & MADDIE: LIFE-SKILL LESSONS THROUGH ROLE-PLAY

10-DIGIT ISBN: 1-57543-139-4
13-DIGIT ISBN: 978-1-57543-139-0

COPYRIGHT © 2006 MAR*CO PRODUCTS, INC.
Published by mar*co products, inc.
1443 Old York Road
Warminster, PA 18974
1-800-448-2197
www.marcoproducts.com

Cover design by Cameon Smith Funk

PERMISSION TO REPRODUCE: The purchaser may reproduce the activity sheets, free and without special permission, for participant use for a particular group or class. Reproduction of these materials for an entire school system is forbidden.

All rights reserved. Except as provided above, no part of this book may be reproduced or transmitted in whole or in part in any form or by any means, electronic or mechanical, including photocopying, recording, or by any information storage or retrieval system without permission in writing from the publisher.

PRINTED IN THE U.S.A.

ABOUT THE AUTHOR

Pat Vargas is a former teacher and counselor. From 1992-2001, she was a counselor at Carlos Rivera Elementary School for the El Paso Independent School District in El Paso, Texas. Prior to that, she instructed gifted/talented fifth-graders and taught in kindergarten, second, third, fifth, and sixth grades for 28 years. She has also worked with college and high school students as a reading instructor at El Paso Community College and at the El Paso Independent District's Evening School. She has served as Master Teacher and director of the Kindergarten Lab and as a developmental reading instructor at The University of Texas at El Paso. In 1985, she earned recognition as one of the El Paso Independent School District's Top Ten Teachers of the Year. In 1998, she was the Partner-in-Education Liaison of the Year.

Pat holds a B.S. in elementary education, a master's in education, and a master's in counseling (K-12). She has kindergarten, gifted/talented, reading specialist, and bilingual certifications. In 1999, Pat became a certified *Character Counts!* trainer and traveled the nation training groups in character education. Pat retired from the El Paso Independent School District in May 2001, and is currently a field specialist for the alternative certification program of the Region 19 Educational Service Center in El Paso. She and her husband have three grown children and two grandchildren, Alex and Maddie.

OTHER MAR∗CO PUBLICATIONS BY PAT VARGAS

Character Cookies
Character Dominoes
Character Cards

DEDICATION

This book is dedicated to Alex, Maddie,
and all children who must make choices
about what to say or do in tough situations and
who base those choices on good character traits.

CONTENTS

NOTES FROM THE AUTHOR

A Note To Students

Life is full of choices, and with choices come positive or negative character-building consequences. The lessons and scenarios in this book give you an opportunity to help Maddie and Alex make choices based on good character traits. You might encounter some of this book's 78 scenarios at home, at school, and in your community. Some of these scenarios are serious. Some are not. The purpose of this book is to have you think, as you help Alex and Maddie choose, about the daily choices that reflect your character. Your challenge is to think about making the right choice for the right reason. By developing this skill, you will learn to think before you do or say anything. If you feel uneasy or uncomfortable about a decision, talk with your parent or another adult whom you trust. Have fun helping Alex and Maddie make choices based on good character traits!

A Message To Parents, Teachers, And Counselors

As children go about their daily activities of growing up and, particularly, interacting with their peers, they must make many choices and deal with peer pressure. The purpose of *Alex & Maddie* is to provide you with scenarios any child might face. The book allows for much interaction between children, teachers, counselors, and/or parents. Use it as a guide to initiate conversation and discussion on different choices in the various scenarios that follow each lesson. The scenario listed under a particular character trait does not necessarily reflect only that character trait.

As you finish each lesson, assign one of the scenarios to a group of students. Tell the students in the group to think about what actions/choices they would advise Alex or Maddie to take. Alex and Maddie have been used in order to take the focus off the children who are using this book. Hopefully, this will give them the freedom to speak without feeling that their choices are being judged.

The scenarios described in this book make ideal topics for discussion. Scenarios may encourage students to describe similar situations they have witnessed or have experienced. In a group setting, these situations can be used in role-playing and cooperative learning. Parts can be assigned and children can create their own dialogue. Follow-up activities are suggested at the end of each lesson.

These scenarios can be used to begin the school day, in a counseling setting at school, to fill final moments at the end of the school day, to initiate conversation at the dinner table, and to pass idle time while traveling.

Children who have had the opportunity to discuss choices in advance will be more apt to choose wisely when confronted with similar situations. By focusing on the character traits of *trustworthiness, respect, responsibility, fairness, caring, citizenship, perseverance,* and *volunteerism*, children may aspire to make the right choices for the right reasons. Hopefully, this will become a lifelong skill.

Introducing The Program

Introduce the program by reproducing *My Character Blooms Garden* and *Flowers* (pages 12-13) for each student. Distribute the activity sheets, crayons, and a folder to each student. Have the students color the garden and the flowers representing the traits you will be presenting. Collect the folders. As each of the character traits is taught, have the students show they understand its meanings by either describing the trait or doing a deed that represents that trait. At that time, return the folders to the students and give them scissors and glue. Tell the students to cut out the flower representing the character trait just taught and glue it to the garden fence. Collect the folders.

Character Awards

The awards found at the end of each unit can be used during and/or after each unit. They are a great way to reinforce and praise students for displaying character reflecting *trustworthiness, respect, responsibility, fairness, caring, citizenship, perseverance,* or *volunteerism.*

Reproduce the award, then place the student's name on the first line. Write a short description of the reason the award is being issued. Be sure to date and sign the award at the bottom.

Sending these awards home is a great way to communicate in a positive manner the character traits that are being stressed at school and to show parents the positive progress their children are making.

Supplementary Activity Sheets

The supplementary activity sheets on pages 221-240 may be used during your presentations or after the units have been taught.

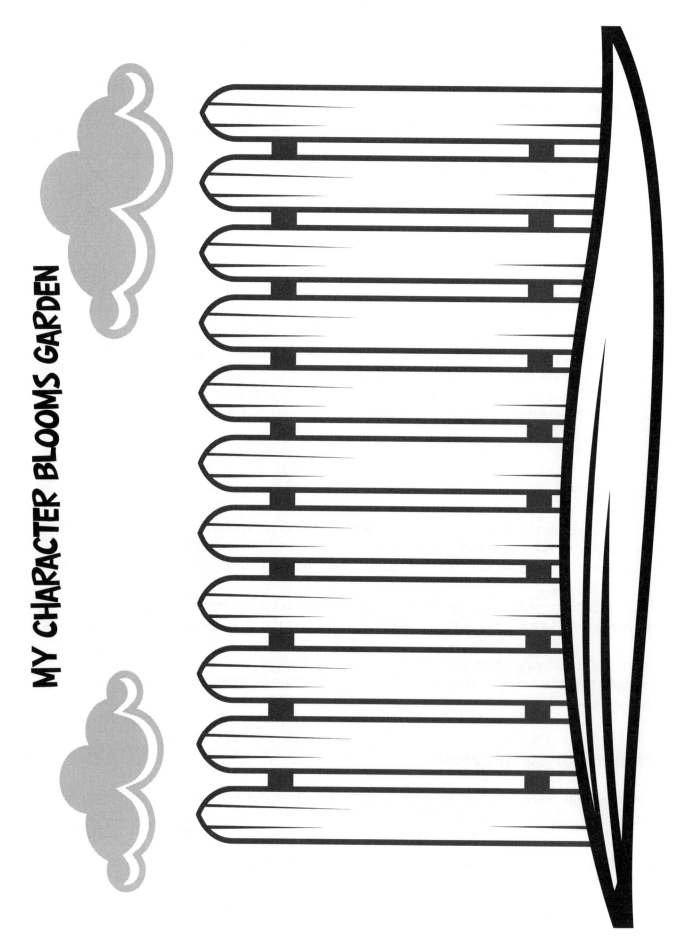

MY CHARACTER BLOOMS GARDEN

ALEX & MADDIE: LIFE-SKILL LESSONS THROUGH ROLE-PLAY © 2006 MAR*CO PRODUCTS, INC. 1-800-448-2197

TOPIC OBJECTIVES

Chapter 1: **TRUSTWORTHINESS**

- Tell the truth.
- Be loyal to your family, friends, school, community, and country.
- Be dependable. Do what you say you will do.
- Don't lie, cheat, or steal.

Chapter 2: **RESPECT**

- Do unto others as you would have them do unto you. Follow *The Golden Rule.*
- Don't threaten, yell at, hit, or hurt another person or an animal.
- Mind your manners and use appropriate language.
- It is okay for people to look different, speak different languages, or dress differently.
- When confronted with anger, bad language, or disagreements, handle them respectfully and peacefully.

Chapter 3: **RESPONSIBILITY**

- Try to always do your very best.
- Remember to think before you act—actions have consequences.
- Don't give up! Keep trying.
- If you are supposed to do something, do it!
- Use self-discipline and self-control.

Chapter 4: **FAIRNESS**

- Share and take turns.
- Listen to others and be open-minded.
- Follow the rules in everything you do.
- Don't blame others if things don't work out.
- Be sure not to take advantage of others or of their trust.

Chapter 5: **CARING**

- Help others in need.
- Show kindness and compassion.
- Forgive others readily.
- Show gratitude to others.

Chapter 6: **CITIZENSHIP**

- Show respect for the United States flag.
- Do your part to make your family, school, and community a better place and to take care of the environment.
- Be informed and vote in school elections.
- Help your neighbors.
- Cooperate.
- Obey rules and laws.

Chapter 7: **PERSEVERANCE**

- Don't give up.
- Keep trying even in the face of defeat.
- See a job through to the end.

Chapter 8: **VOLUNTEERISM**

- Offer to help others without expecting anything in return.
- Perform a service at home, at school, or in the community, just because you want to do it.
- Volunteer your talents/time to benefit others.

TRUSTWORTHINESS

Topic Objectives:

To help children realize the value of:

Telling the truth.

Loyalty to family, friends, school, community, and country.

Being dependable—doing what you say you will do.

Not lying, cheating, or stealing.

TRUSTWORTHINESS
INTRODUCTION

Purpose:

To help students understand the meaning of *trustworthiness*

Materials Needed:

For the leader:
- ☐ Chart paper and marker
- ☐ Masking tape
- ☐ Dictionary (optional)

For each student:
- None

Pre-Presentation Preparation:

None

Procedure:

▸ Introduce the topic by having the students define, in their own words, what *trustworthy* means to them. Guide the students to a definition.

> Possible examples: A trustworthy person does not lie, cheat, or steal. Someone you can trust. Someone who is honest.

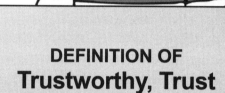

DEFINITION OF
Trustworthy, Trust

Trustworthy: reliable, truthful, honest, dependable, deserving trust

Trust: to have faith in, to believe, to rely on, to confide in, to have complete faith and assurance regarding the character, ability, strength, or truth of someone or something

▸ After the students have agreed on a class definition of *trustworthy,* write the definition on chart paper and post the paper in a place in the classroom where everyone can see it for future reference. The students may want to revise or add to the definition as the lessons on trustworthiness progress. You may give them the definition found above or the dictionary definition. Compare their definition to the formal definition. Make any changes the students or you believe are necessary at this time.

ONE LIE LEADS TO ANOTHER

Purpose:

The students will think about and discuss the importance of telling the truth even when doing so can have unpleasant consequences. Students will see how one lie leads to more lies and makes matters worse. After reading or role-playing the scenarios about telling the truth, the students will have the opportunity to apply what they have learned by helping Alex and Maddie make decisions based on good character traits.

Materials Needed:

For the leader:
- ☐ Chart paper and marker or chalkboard and chalk
- ☐ Large container of water and rock (optional)
- ☐ Dominoes (optional)

For each student:
- ☐ Copy of *Scenario #1* (optional, page 24)
- ☐ Copy of *Scenario #2* (optional, page 25)
- ☐ Copy of *Scenario #3* (optional, page 26)
- ☐ Copy of *Scenario #4* (optional, page 27)
- ☐ Paper (optional)
- ☐ Pencil (optional)

Pre-Presentation Preparation:

Optional: Fill the container with water and place it in a location where the students can gather around and see the ripple effects one lie can have.

Optional: Line up the dominoes so that with one push (one lie) the "domino effect" will occur.

Optional: Make a copy of the chosen scenarios for each student or for each student group.

Procedure:

Note: This lesson may be presented during one or more class periods.

▸ Begin the lesson by asking the students:

Does anyone know what it means to be an honest person? (Allow for student discussion. Write the students' responses on the chalkboard or chart paper.)

What is a lie? (*A lie* is when someone does not tell the truth.)

Have you ever been lied to? (Accept all responses.)

How did it feel? (Accept all responses.)

Have you ever noticed that one lie often seems to lead to another? (Yes.)

▸ Continue the lesson by saying:

Let's play a game showing how one lie leads to another. I will describe a scenario. Then we will go around the classroom, adding to the lie and making the lie bigger.

▸ Read the following aloud:

Maddie had a bad habit of losing many of her possessions—her books, her reading glasses, her pencils, her purse, and lots of other things. One day, Maddie's mother bought her a pretty denim jacket for school. The very first day Maddie wore her jacket to school, she took it off to wash her hands in the girls' restroom and forgot to pick it up. It was not until she was riding the bus home from school that she realized she didn't have it any more.

▸ Stop the story and ask the students to add to the scenario by not telling the truth to Maddie's mother. After hearing each lie, the leader (role-playing Maddie's mother) should ask a question which will lead the next volunteer to make up another lie. Go from volunteer to volunteer, adding to the first lie, showing the students how one lie can lead to another.

▸ For additional examples of one lie leading to another introduce one or both of the following activities.

OPTIONAL ACTIVITY 1:

Drop a rock into the center of a container filled with water. Let the students see how the rock makes ripples. Tell the children that the rock is *a lie* and, as a lie, it sends ripples out into the water. Those ripples cause more lies, which only make matters worse.

OPTIONAL ACTIVITY 2:

Stand the dominoes on end. Tip the first domino and point out the ripple effect that occurs as each domino knocks down the one in front of it. Tell the students that the first domino is a *lie* and the ripple effect that occurs as one domino after the other falls is the same ripple effect that one lie will have.

▸ Have the students begin the scenario again. This time, have Maddie immediately tell the truth. Then ask the students:

   How do you think Maddie felt in the first scenario? In the second scenario? (Accept all appropriate responses.)

   In which scenario would Maddie feel better about herself? (The scenario in which she told the truth.)

▸ If time permits, you may begin the scenarios (pages 24-27) now or you may present the scenarios during a subsequent class period.

▸ Introduce the scenarios by saying:

   Let's look at the role-plays and see if we can guide Alex and Maddie by using what we know about telling the truth.

SCENARIO SUGGESTIONS:

1. Choose one or more scenarios. Read each chosen scenario to the students. Allow time for discussion after each scenario. Continue the discussion as long as the students offer choices and guidance for Maddie and Alex.

2. Divide the class into groups. Have each group role-play a different scenario illustrating choices based on good character traits. Allow time for discussion after each role-play.

3. Have the students read each scenario. After each scenario has been read, use the following questions to stimulate class discussion.

SUGGESTED SCENARIO DISCUSSION QUESTIONS:

Scenario #1

1. ***What is the dilemma or problem that Maddie is facing?*** (Maddie has to decide if she is willing to lie to protect a friend.)

2. ***What are Maddie's choices?*** (She can tell the truth or she can tell a lie.)

3. ***Have you ever been in a similar situation? How did you handle the problem? Was that a good decision?*** (Accept all appropriate responses. Remind the students that the lesson's topic is that telling the truth is the good character trait.)

4. ***Can Maddie tell the truth and still keep Maria as a friend?*** (Yes.) ***How?*** (She can tell the truth and later explain to Maria that she had to do the right thing. Accept all other appropriate responses.)

Scenario #2

1. ***What is the dilemma or problem that Alex is facing?*** (Alex has to decide whether to tell his mother the truth about how the lamp was broken.)

2. ***What are Alex's choices?*** (Alex can tell the truth or make up a lie and place the blame on Maddie.)

3. ***Have you ever been in a situation like this? What did you do? Do you think you made a good decision?*** (Accept all appropriate responses. Keep the students on the topic of telling the truth.)

4. ***If Alex asked you for advice, what would you advise him to say or do?*** (Telling a lie is never the right thing to do. You will not feel good about yourself, and one lie often leads to another. Accept all other appropriate responses.)

Scenario #3

1. ***What is the dilemma or problem that Alex is facing?*** (Alex does not want Bobby to be expelled.)

2. ***What are Alex's choices?*** (He can tell Coach Vargas the truth or he can make up a story [lie] to cover up for Bobby.)

3. ***Have you ever had a friend who asked you to lie for him/her? How did you feel? What did you do?*** (Accept all appropriate responses. Keep the students on the topic of telling the truth.)

4. ***What should Alex choose to say or do?*** (Alex should tell Coach Vargas the truth. Accept all other appropriate responses.)

Scenario #4

1. ***What is the dilemma or problem that Maddie is facing?*** (Maddie does not want to get into trouble for not bringing her homework to class.)

2. ***What are Maddie's choices?*** (To tell the truth and simply say that she forgot to take her textbooks home or lie so she doesn't get into trouble with the teacher.)

3. *Has this ever happened to you? What did you do? Was it a good choice?* (Accept all appropriate responses that reinforce the concept that telling the truth is the good choice.)

4. *What should Maddie choose to say or do?* (Maddie should tell her teacher the truth. Accept all other appropriate responses that help guide Maddie to choose the good character trait of telling the truth.)

Follow-Up Activities:

▸ When the discussion of the scenarios has been completed, ask the students:

What do you think about telling the truth? (Accept all appropriate responses.)

Is it hard to tell the truth? Do you think telling the truth can get you into more trouble? (Accept all appropriate responses.)

Are there any times when you should not tell the truth? (Accept all appropriate responses.)

Sometimes telling the truth is hard. Why is it always better than telling a lie or hiding the truth? (Encourage discussion of all the responses.)

▸ Conclude the discussion by asking:

Have you heard the saying, "One lie leads to another?" Once we tell that first lie, we often have to tell more lies to protect the first lie, and the truth will eventually catch up with us. When people find out that you lied, they will be less likely to believe you the next time you say something. You've heard the saying "Once a liar, always a liar."

▸ Give each student paper and a pencil. Have the students write original scenarios on the topic of telling the truth.

SCENARIO #1

Maria and Rebecca get into a pushing match during a kickball game during lunchtime recess. Maria started it by making fun of Rebecca and pushing her. Mr. Vargas, the P.E. coach, comes over to settle the disturbance. Mr. Vargas asks Maddie and a few other students to tell him what they saw. Maria is Maddie's friend and Maddie does not want to get Maria into trouble. However, Maddie knows that Maria really caused the whole problem.

What should Maddie choose to say or do?

 ALEX & MADDIE: LIFE-SKILL LESSONS THROUGH ROLE-PLAY © 2006 MAR∗CO PRODUCTS, INC. 1-800-448-2197

SCENARIO #2

Alex and his little sister, Maddie, begin wrestling at home one afternoon after school. Their mother is not home. It is fun until they knock over their mother's favorite lamp and break it. Alex knows he and Maddie are not supposed to play rough in the house. It would be very easy to place all of the blame on Maddie. Alex really doesn't want to get into trouble. He thinks that his mother will be more understanding if she thinks Maddie just "accidentally broke the lamp."

What should Alex choose to say or do?

SCENARIO #3

During the last few days of school, stink bombs have been thrown in the hall and bathrooms. As Coach Vargas enters the boys restroom in the upper-grade hall, Bobby and Alex are coming out. Bobby has just popped a stink bomb that he brought to school. Coach Vargas notices the smell and sees the remains of the stink bomb on the floor. There are no other boys in the restroom. He calls Bobby and Alex back. Neither Bobby nor Alex wants to admit who popped the stink bomb. Coach sends both boys to the office. On the way to the office, Bobby asks Alex to say he was the one who brought the stink bomb to school. This is Bobby's third offense. If the principal finds out he is guilty, Bobby will be expelled and sent to an alternative school. Bobby is one of Alex's friends. If Alex doesn't take the blame, he will not see Bobby for the rest of the year.

What should Alex choose to say or do?

ALEX & MADDIE: LIFE-SKILL LESSONS THROUGH ROLE-PLAY © 2006 MAR*CO PRODUCTS, INC. 1-800-448-2197

SCENARIO #4

Maddie has been very conscientious, doing her homework all year and turning it in on time. Maddie has noticed that some of the other students don't seem to work as hard as she does and often forget to do their homework or to bring it to class. The teacher seems to give them more time or more chances to turn in their work. Maddie didn't do any of her homework last night, because she forgot to take home the necessary books. When her teacher begins collecting all the completed homework assignments, Maddie doesn't have hers. She could make up a story about having an emergency at home last night.

What should Maddie choose to say or do?

STEALING

Purpose:

The students will learn how it feels to have something of importance or value taken from them. Students will learn that *stealing* is more than just taking something from someone and facing the possibility of being caught and punished. After reading or role-playing the scenarios, the students will demonstrate their understanding of applying good character choices by helping Alex and Maddie make good decisions.

DEFINITION OF
Stealing

Stealing: taking another's possession illegally and without his/her knowledge, obtaining something without permission

Materials Needed:

For the leader:
- ☐ Chart paper and marker or chalkboard and chalk
- ☐ Dictionary
- ☐ Newspapers (optional)

For each student:
- ☐ 3 note cards
- ☐ Pencil
- ☐ Copy of *Scenario #5* (optional, page 33)
- ☐ Copy of *Scenario #6* (optional, page 34)
- ☐ Copy of *Scenario #7* (optional, page 35)
- ☐ Copy of *Scenario #8* (optional, page 36)
- ☐ Copy of *Scenario #9* (optional, page 37)
- ☐ Paper (optional)

Pre-Presentation Preparation:

Optional: Make a copy of the chosen scenarios for each student or for each student group.

Procedure:

Note: This lesson may be presented during one or more class periods.

▸ Ask the students to define *stealing* for the class. Write these definitions on the chalkboard or chart paper. After writing down several definitions, have a student look up the definition of stealing in the dictionary.

▸ Ask the students the following questions:

Have you or your family ever had something stolen? (Accept all appropriate responses.)

How did having something stolen from you make you feel? (Accept all appropriate responses.)

▸ Distribute three note cards and a pencil to each student. Then say:

On each note card, write one possession that is very important to you. Also write why each of these three things is important to you.

Turn the cards over and shuffle them around on your desk. On the back of one of the cards, draw a large X.

This is the possession that will be taken from you. Turn the card over and see what has been stolen from you.

▸ Ask the following questions:

How did it feel to have something that meant so much to you taken from you? (Accept all appropriate responses.)

If having something stolen from you made you angry or sad, would you feel guilty about taking something from someone and making that person feel angry or sad? (Accept all appropriate responses.)

Do you think that the thief knows how special this item was/is to you? (Probably not. Accept all appropriate responses.)

What would you like to tell the thief? (Accept all appropriate responses.)

▸ If time permits, you may begin the scenarios (pages 33-37) now or you may present the scenarios during a subsequent class period.

▸ Introduce the scenarios by saying:

Let's look at the role-plays and see if we can guide Alex and Maddie by using what we know about taking things that do not belong to us.

SCENARIO SUGGESTIONS:

1. Choose one or more scenarios. Read each chosen scenario to the students. Allow time for discussion after each scenario. Continue the discussion as long as the students offer choices and guidance for Maddie and Alex.

2. Divide the class into groups. Have each group role-play a different scenario illustrating choices based on good character traits. Allow time for discussion after each role-play.

3. Have the students read each scenario. After each scenario has been read, use the following questions to stimulate class discussion.

SUGGESTED SCENARIO DISCUSSION QUESTIONS:

Scenario #5

1. ***What is the problem or dilemma that Maddie is facing?*** (Maddie really likes that bracelet. Should she return it to Rebecca or make another choice?)

2. ***What are Maddie's choices?*** (Maddie could keep the bracelet. She could return the bracelet to Rebecca. She could turn it in to Lost and Found and hope that Rebecca never claims it and it then becomes Maddie's. She could hide the bracelet and come back for it later.)

3. ***Have you ever found something you wanted to keep? What choice did you make? Do you feel that you made the right decision?*** (Accept all appropriate responses. Keep the students on the topic of making good choices and emphasize that stealing and lying are never good choices.)

4. ***If you find something and keep it even though you know who it belongs to, is that stealing?*** (Yes, absolutely.)

5. ***What should Maddie choose to say or do?*** (Maddie should return the bracelet to Rebecca. That would be the honest and trustworthy thing to do. It would be a win-win situation. Rebecca would feel good and Maddie would feel good about herself for doing the right thing. Accept all other appropriate responses.)

Scenario #6

1. ***What is the problem or dilemma that Alex is facing?*** (Is Alex willing to steal a candy bar?)

2. ***Is there more than one dilemma or problem in this scenario?*** (Yes. Is Alex willing to do anything to keep a friend—such as stealing, lying, etc.?)

3. ***What are Alex's choices?*** (Alex can say *no* to Johnny. Alex can steal the candy bar. Alex can just go home and say nothing.)

4. ***Have you ever been in a similar situation? What did you choose to say or do? Was it a good decision?*** (Accept all appropriate responses. Keep the students on the topic of not stealing under any circumstances.)

5. ***What could you say to Alex to help him sort out his choices?*** (Stealing is never right under any circumstances. If Johnny is testing Alex's friendship, maybe Johnny is not such a good friend to have.)

6. ***What should Alex choose to say or do?*** (Alex should definitely not steal the candy bar. He should tell Johnny stealing is wrong. Accept all other appropriate responses.)

Scenario #7

1. ***What is the problem or dilemma that Maddie is facing?*** (Maddie does not want to get into trouble with the teacher or her parents for losing her textbook.)

2. ***What are Maddie's choices?*** (Maddie can tell the truth. She can lie and say that her book was stolen. She can take Brenda's book.)

3. ***Would Maddie be doing something besides stealing if she took Brenda's book?*** (Yes. She would also be lying, because she is saying that Brenda's book is hers.)

4. ***Have you ever been in a situation in which you were afraid to admit to your parents or teacher that you had lost something? How did you handle the situation? Was it a good choice?*** (Accept all appropriate responses. Keep the students on the topic of making good choices and emphasize that stealing and lying are never good choices.)

5. ***What should Maddie choose to say or do?*** (Maddie should tell the truth. She can offer to do chores to earn the money to pay for the book. Telling the truth will also make Maddie feel good about herself. It is the choice a trustworthy person would make. Accept all other appropriate responses.)

Scenario #8

1. ***What is the temptation that Alex is facing?*** (Those dollar bills are awfully inviting. Alex could sure use the extra money.)

2. ***What are Alex's choices?*** (Alex can take the money. He can let the teacher know that her purse is open and things are falling out of it. He can just keep quiet.)

3. ***Have you or anyone you know been in a similar situation? How was it handled? Was that a good decision?*** (Accept all appropriate responses. Keep the students on the topic of making good choices and emphasize that stealing is never a good choice.)

4. ***What can Alex say to guide himself to a decision based on good character traits?*** (He can remind himself that stealing is never a good idea. Alex can also ask himself, "If that were my mom's purse, wouldn't I like a student to let her know that money was falling out of it?")

5. *What should Alex choose to say or do?* (Alex should let the teacher know that her purse is open and things are falling out of it. Accept all other appropriate responses.)

Scenario #9

1. *What is the temptation that Maddie is facing?* (Maddie needs money to spend at the School Store and she sees money lying on the ground.)

2. *What are Maddie's choices?* (She can quietly pick up some of the money that looks like it might blow away and keep it as her own. She can do nothing. She can let an adult know that money is likely to blow away. If she knows who the money belongs to, she can warn those students that their money is ready to be blown away by the wind.)

3. *Have you ever been in a similar situation? How did you handle it? Was that a good decision?* (Accept all appropriate responses. Keep the students on the topic of making good choices and emphasize that stealing and lying are never good choices.)

4. *What can Maddie say to guide herself to a decision based on good character traits?* (She could ask herself if she would rather have someone take her money or warn her that her money might be blown away. She could remind herself that stealing is never a good choice and that she will not feel good about herself if she steals.)

5. *What should Maddie choose to say or do?* (Maddie should let an adult know that money is likely to blow away. If she knows who the money belongs to, she should warn those students that their money is ready to be blown away by the wind. Accept all other appropriate responses.)

Follow-Up Activities:

▶ Say:

> *If you are ever tempted to take someone else's property without asking permission, please remember what we have discussed in this lesson. Remember to think things through before you act on an impulse and always remember to think about how you would feel if someone took something that belonged to you.*

▶ Give each student paper. Have the students write original scenarios depicting how stealing hurts all of us.

> Example: Shoplifting—The consumer ends up paying for theft because prices are increased by the store to offset the losses caused by shoplifting.

▶ Students may work in pairs or small groups to find examples of stealing in local newspaper articles.

SCENARIO #5

Rebecca has a bracelet Maddie has liked ever since Rebecca got it for her birthday. One day, Maddie finds the bracelet on the floor in a stall in the girls' restroom. The bracelet is simply gorgeous and Maddie knows exactly who it belongs to.

What should Maddie choose to say or do?

SCENARIO #6

Alex and Johnny are walking home after school and stop at the small convenience store on the corner. Alex has already spent his allowance for the week and knows that he has no money left to spend. Johnny has just enough money for a candy bar. Johnny has an idea. If he distracts the cashier with his transaction, Alex can quietly slip a candy bar into his pocket. Alex feels very uneasy about this, but he really likes Johnny and doesn't want Johnny to think he is a "chicken." Besides, a candy bar sounds pretty yummy.

What should Alex choose to say or do?

ALEX & MADDIE: LIFE-SKILL LESSONS THROUGH ROLE-PLAY © 2006 MAR★CO PRODUCTS, INC. 1-800-448-2197

SCENARIO #7

Maddie lost her math book recently and the teacher is getting ready for a "book check." Maddie does not have the money to pay for the book and she knows her parents will be very upset with her for being so irresponsible. Maddie sits near Brenda, who has not put her name in any of her textbooks. Brenda always seems to have money, so it would be no problem for her to pay for a lost textbook. Maddie thinks Brenda probably won't even notice for a while that her math book is missing. Brenda tends to be even more disorganized than Maddie.

What should Maddie choose to say or do?

SCENARIO #8

Alex's class is very involved in a creative project. The teacher is going from group to group, guiding the students. When she gets to Alex's group, she asks Alex to go to her desk and bring her a stapler. Alex quickly goes to the teacher's desk and gets the stapler. He notices that the teacher's purse is open and a few dollar bills are hanging out. She is a teacher. She has lots of money. Would she even miss a few dollar bills? If Alex doesn't take the money, it is possible that someone else in the class will.

What should Alex choose to say or do?

ALEX & MADDIE: LIFE-SKILL LESSONS THROUGH ROLE-PLAY © 2006 MAR*CO PRODUCTS, INC. 1-800-448-2197

SCENARIO #9

Every morning, some students at Maddie's school place their lunch money on the ground to hold their spot in line while they play games. The money is always still there when they finish playing. The School Store will be open at lunch today and Maddie forgot to bring money to buy some items. It is a little windy and Maddie notices that some of the money is beginning to move slightly. Maddie could sure use some of that money to spend at the School Store. The students who put it there always have money, so they would be able to "charge" their lunch with no problem. Everyone would just think the wind has blown the money away.

What should Maddie choose to say or do?

TRUSTWORTHINESS: LESSON 3
CHEATING

Purpose:

The students will give their definition of *cheating* and compare their definitions with the one in the dictionary. The students will cite personal examples of cheating. After reading or role-playing the scenarios, the students will help guide Alex and Maddie to make decisions based on good character traits.

Materials Needed:

For the leader:
- ☐ Masking tape
- ☐ Dictionary (optional)

For each student:
- ☐ Copy of *Scenario #10* (optional, page 41)
- ☐ Copy of *Scenario #11* (optional, page 42)
- ☐ Paper (optional)
- ☐ Pencil (optional)

For each student group:
- ☐ Piece of chart paper
- ☐ Marker

DEFINITION OF
Cheating

Cheating: Tricking or deceiving someone, such as obtaining something (such as money) or taking advantage of someone by dishonest behavior

Pre-Presentation Preparation:

Optional: Make a copy of the chosen scenarios for each student or for each student group.

Procedure:

Note: This lesson may be presented during one or more class periods.

▸ Divide the class into groups. Be sure to break up any cliques and try to balance the number of boys and girls in each group. Distribute a piece of chart paper and marker to each group and have each group select a reporter. The reporter will write the group's responses on a piece of chart paper. (These posters will be displayed for future discussion.)

▸ Ask the groups to define *cheating* and to list as many examples of cheating as they can think of. Allow approximately 10 minutes to complete this part of the lesson. Have the group reporter report its group's findings. Compare the students' definition of *cheating* to the definition on page 38 or the dictionary definition. Post the students' definitions and examples in the classroom.

▸ If time permits, you may begin the scenarios (pages 41-42) now or you may present the scenarios during a subsequent class period.

▸ Introduce the scenarios by saying:

Let's look at the role-plays and see if we can guide Alex and Maddie by using what we know about responding to situations involving cheating.

SCENARIO SUGGESTIONS:

1. Choose one or more scenarios. Read each chosen scenario to the students. Allow time for discussion after each scenario. Continue the discussion as long as the students offer choices and guidance for Maddie and Alex.

2. Divide the class into groups. Have each group role-play a different scenario illustrating choices based on good character traits. Allow time for discussion after each role-play.

3. Have the students read each scenario. After each scenario has been read, use the following questions to stimulate class discussion.

SUGGESTED SCENARIO DISCUSSION QUESTIONS:

Scenario #10

1. *What is the dilemma or problem that Maddie is facing?* (Is Maddie willing to cheat in order to help a friend?)

2. *Would Maddie really be helping Lucy by allowing her to copy from her paper?* (Absolutely not. Allow the students to elaborate on this.)

3. *What are Maddie's choices?* (Maddie can ignore Lucy. Maddie can position the paper so Lucy can copy her responses. Maddie can tell the teacher. Maddie can say *no*. Maddie can say *no* and later talk with Lucy about cheating.)

4. *How would Maddie feel about herself and her own trustworthiness if she allowed Lucy to copy her responses?* (Maddie would be disappointed and angry with herself for being so weak. She should not have to make a bad choice in order to keep a friend. Maddie could feel guilty about cheating and not being trustworthy.)

5. *What could Maddie say to Lucy?* (She could say *no* to Lucy and later explain that this is not the way a trustworthy person acts. Accept all appropriate responses. Keep students on the topic of trustworthiness and not cheating.)

6. *In the future, how could Maddie really help Lucy?* (Since Maddie knows that Lucy has trouble in this subject, perhaps she can offer to study with her before the test. Accept all appropriate responses.)

7. *What should Maddie choose to say or do?* (Maddie should not allow Lucy to copy from her paper. Accept all other appropriate responses.)

Scenario #11

1. *What is the dilemma or problem that Alex is facing?* (Alex wants to keep Sean as a friend. Should he allow Sean to copy his homework?)

2. *Is letting someone copy your homework responses really cheating?* (Yes, absolutely. Allow the students to elaborate on this.)

3. *What are Alex's choices?* (Alex could let Sean copy his work. He could say *no*. He could pretend that he didn't hear Sean ask to copy his homework.)

4. *What could Alex say to Sean?* ("Sean, I was up late last night finishing my homework and I learned a lot by doing it. It would be better for you if you did it yourself." Accept all appropriate responses.)

5. *What should Alex choose to say or do?* (Alex should not allow Sean to copy his homework. Accept all other appropriate responses.)

Follow-Up Activities:

▸ Ask the students:

Is it cheating to ask a friend to give you the responses to a homework assignment?

How will you answer when that friend asks to copy your responses?

Remember that all choices have consequences. Think carefully before you help someone cheat. Are you really doing a favor when you help someone cheat? Why or why not?

▸ Give each student paper and a pencil. Have the students write original scenarios on *cheating*.

▸ Revisit the students' definition of *trustworthy* and see if the students feel a need to revise, add to, or change it.

SCENARIO #10

It is test time at the end of the grading period. Maddie feels pretty confident because she has paid attention in class and has kept up with her homework. Lucy, Maddie's best friend, has been goofing off all this time. Lucy is in Maddie's class and sits right behind her. Lucy is very stressed and finally asks Maddie if she will turn her test paper so Lucy can see her responses. Maddie knows this is not the right thing to do. Maddie really likes Lucy and would like very much to help her.

What should Maddie choose to say or do?

SCENARIO #11

Soccer practice last night took longer than usual. The next morning, Sean asked Alex if he could copy the responses to the math homework. Alex had stayed up quite late to finish it himself. Is letting someone share your homework responses really cheating?

What should Alex choose to say or do?

ALEX & MADDIE: LIFE-SKILL LESSONS THROUGH ROLE-PLAY © 2006 MAR*CO PRODUCTS, INC. 1-800-448-2197

TRUSTWORTHINESS

_____

was caught showing
good character when
displaying *trustworthiness* by

_____

_____

_____

Date _____

Signature _____

RESPECT

Topic Objectives:

To help children realize the value of:

Doing unto others as you would have them do unto you—
following The Golden Rule.

Not threatening, yelling at, hitting, or hurting another person or animal.

Minding their manners and using appropriate language.

Understanding that it is okay for people to look different,
speak different languages, or dress differently.

Respectfully and peacefully handling situations involving
anger, confrontation, bad language, or disagreements.

RESPECT
INTRODUCTION

Purpose:

To help students understand the meaning of *respect*

Materials Needed:

For the leader:
- ☐ Chart paper and marker
- ☐ Masking tape
- ☐ Dictionary (optional)

For each student:
- None

Pre-Presentation Preparation:

None

DEFINITION OF
Respect, Respectful

Respect: the special esteem or consideration in which one holds another person or thing, to admire, revere, esteem

Respectful: showing respect

Procedure:

▸ Introduce the topic by having the students define, in their own words, what *respect* means to them. Guide the students to a definition.

> Possible examples: A person shows respect by acting nice and polite to other people. A person who is respectful is not mean. Respectful people use polite words like *please; thank you; may I; no, Ma'am; yes, Ma'am; no, Sir; yes, Sir;* etc.

▸ After the students have agreed on a class definition of *respect,* write the definition on chart paper and post the paper in a place in the classroom where everyone can see it for future reference. The students may want to revise or add to the definition as the lessons on respect progress. You may give them the definition found above or the dictionary definition. Compare their definition to the formal definition. Make any changes the students or you believe are necessary at this time.

THE GOLDEN RULE

Purpose:

The students will learn that respect should be shown to everyone—celebrities, heroes, athletes, elders, those in authority, peers, family, friends, etc. The students will learn *The Golden Rule* and what it means. After reading or role-playing the scenarios, the students will apply their knowledge of *The Golden Rule* and help guide Alex and Maddie through several situations.

Materials Needed:

For the leader:
- ☐ Chart paper and marker or chalkboard and chalk

For each student:
- ☐ Copy of *My Golden Ruler* (optional, page 51)
- ☐ Copy of *Scenario #12* (optional, page 52)
- ☐ Copy of *Scenario #13* (optional, page 53)
- ☐ Copy of *Scenario #14* (optional, page 54)
- ☐ Pencil (optional)
- ☐ Scissors (optional)
- ☐ Gluestick (optional)
- ☐ Paper (optional)

Pre-Presentation Preparation:

Write *The Golden Rule—Do unto others as you would have them do unto you*—and its translation—*Treat others the way you would like to be treated*—on the chart paper/chalkboard.

Reproduce *My Golden Ruler* on gold or yellow cardstock for each student.

Optional: Make a copy of the chosen scenarios for each student or for each student group.

Procedure:

Note: This lesson may be presented during one or more class periods.

▸ Begin by asking the students to read the definition of *The Golden Rule.* (For lower grades, read the definition to the class.)

► Then ask the students:

What do you think The Golden Rule *means*? (Accept all responses that show the students understand that *The Golden Rule* means treating others the way we would want to be treated.)

Compliment the students on knowing that *The Golden Rule* simply means that you want others to be nice to you, so you are nice to others.

► If time permits, you may begin the scenarios (pages 52-54) now or you may present the scenarios during a subsequent class period.

► Introduce the scenarios by saying:

Let's look at the role-plays and see if we can guide Alex and Maddie by using what we know about The Golden Rule.

SCENARIO SUGGESTIONS:

1. Choose one or more scenarios. Read each chosen scenario to the students. Allow time for discussion after each scenario. Continue the discussion as long as the students offer choices and guidance for Maddie and Alex.

2. Divide the class into groups. Have each group role-play a different scenario illustrating choices based on good character traits. Allow time for discussion after each role-play.

3. Have the students read each scenario. After each scenario has been read, use the following questions to stimulate class discussion.

SUGGESTED SCENARIO DISCUSSION QUESTIONS:

Scenario #12

1. **What is the dilemma or problem that Maddie is facing?** (Maddie does not know whether to go along with the class and be disrespectful to Mrs. Ray or to follow *The Golden Rule*.)

2. **What are Maddie's choices?** (Maddie can join the class and call Mrs. Ray "Scar Face." Maddie can do nothing. Maddie can talk with some of the students who started this and tell them it is wrong and that they should quit. Maddie could tell her teacher. Maddie could talk with her parents.)

3. ***Has this ever happened to you? How did you handle it? Do you feel that you did the right thing and followed*** **The Golden Rule?** (Accept all appropriate responses. Keep the students on the topic of following *The Golden Rule.*)

4. ***What should Maddie choose to say or do?*** (Maddie should follow *The Golden Rule.* Accept all other appropriate responses.)

Scenario #13

1. ***What is the problem or dilemma that Alex is facing?*** (Alex doesn't know whether to join his classmates who are making fun of the custodian.)

2. ***What are Alex's choices?*** (Alex can follow *The Golden Rule* and be respectful of the custodian. He can tell an adult. He can make fun of the custodian himself.)

3. ***Have you ever been in a similar situation? How did you handle it? Was that a good choice?*** (Accept all appropriate responses. Keep the students on the topic of following *The Golden Rule.*)

4. ***What should Alex choose to say or do?*** (Alex should follow *The Golden Rule.* He could speak with an adult about the situation. He could remind the other students that this is very disrespectful behavior. Accept all other appropriate responses.)

Scenario #14

1. ***What is Maddie's dilemma or problem with Jennifer?*** (Jennifer is not following *The Golden Rule.* She is being very disrespectful and mean to Maddie.)

2. ***What are Maddie's choices?*** (Maddie needs to have respect for herself and let Jennifer know that this is unacceptable behavior. Maddie can speak with her parents or another adult about the problem. Maddie can do nothing and just keep everything as it is. Maddie can find another friend.)

3. ***Has a friend ever treated you this way? What did you do? Was that the best way to handle the situation?*** (Accept all appropriate responses. Keep the students on the topic of following *The Golden Rule.*)

4. ***What should Maddie choose to say or do?*** (Maddie needs to respect herself and tell Jennifer to stop treating her this way or they can no longer be friends. Maddie should speak with her parents or another adult whom she trusts. Accept all other appropriate responses.)

Follow-Up Activities:

▸ Say:

> *Whenever you are tempted to be disrespectful or mean, remember this lesson on* The Golden Rule *and ask yourself, "How would I feel if I were treated in the disrespectful, mean way I am tempted to treat this person?" Remember that we need to treat others as we would like to be treated ourselves.*

▸ Give each student paper and a pencil. Have the students write original scenarios on applying *The Golden Rule* in their own lives.

▸ Distribute *My Golden Ruler,* scissors, a gluestick, and a pencil to each student. Have the students write their names on the ruler, cut the ruler out, fold it, and glue the triangle. Tell the students to keep the ruler in a prominent place either at their desks or in their binders to help remind them to be respectful of others.

MY GOLDEN RULER

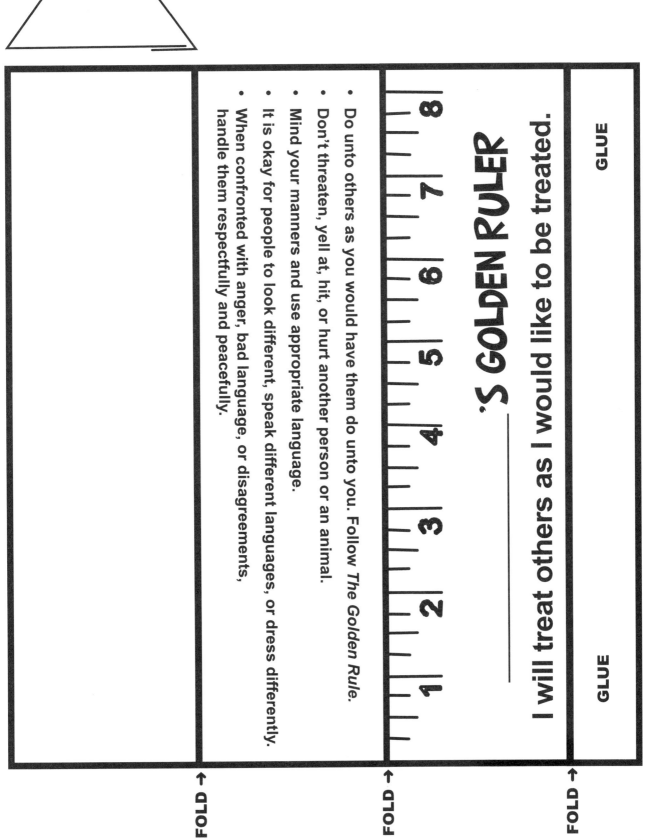

____'S GOLDEN RULER

I will treat others as I would like to be treated.

- Do unto others as you would have them do unto you. Follow *The Golden Rule.*
- Don't threaten, yell at, hit, or hurt another person or an animal.
- Mind your manners and use appropriate language.
- It is okay for people to look different, speak different languages, or dress differently.
- When confronted with anger, bad language, or disagreements, handle them respectfully and peacefully.

GLUE

GLUE

FOLD →

FOLD →

FOLD →

SCENARIO #12

Maddie's teacher, Mrs. Ray, has a small scar on her left cheek. It is somewhat noticeable. Some of Maddie's classmates have decided to call Mrs. Ray "Scar Face" behind her back. It started with just a few students, but the word has spread and now most of the class is doing it. The students seem to think it is very funny. When the students refer to Mrs. Ray before class—and even sometimes in class without her hearing—they call the teacher, "Scar Face." Maddie likes her teacher and feels uncomfortable doing this.

What should Maddie choose to say or do?

 ALEX & MADDIE: LIFE-SKILL LESSONS THROUGH ROLE-PLAY © 2006 MAR*CO PRODUCTS, INC. 1-800-448-2197

SCENARIO #13

Some of the students in Alex's classroom enjoy making fun of the custodian who cleans different areas around the school. It has gotten to the point that they now hide his cleaning tools and supplies when he is not looking. Alex has not participated in these activities so far, but he is feeling pressured to do so by some of his classmates.

What should Alex choose to say or do?

SCENARIO #14

Jennifer calls Maddie her very best friend. Maddie likes Jennifer, too. Over time, however, Jennifer has begun making fun of Maddie and putting her down. Jennifer particularly enjoys doing this in front of all the other girls. When Maddie asks about this, Jennifer tells her to "get over it." Maddie enjoys the idea of having a best friend, but wonders if Jennifer is really a friend at all.

What should Maddie choose to say or do?

ALEX & MADDIE: LIFE-SKILL LESSONS THROUGH ROLE-PLAY © 2006 MAR∗CO PRODUCTS, INC. 1-800-448-2197

DISPLAYING ANGER INAPPROPRIATELY

Purpose:

The students will see how losing their tempers and saying and doing things impulsively cannot be changed. After reading or role-playing the scenarios, the students will apply their understanding of displaying anger inappropriately by guiding Alex and Maddie through several situations.

Materials Needed:

For the leader:
- ☐ Option #1: a paper plate and a tube of toothpaste
- ☐ Option #2: a paper plate and a container of shaving cream

For each student:
- ☐ Copy of *Scenario #15* (optional, page 58)
- ☐ Copy of *Scenario #16* (optional, page 59)
- ☐ Paper (optional)
- ☐ Pencil (optional)

Pre-Presentation Preparation:

Optional: Make a copy of the chosen scenarios for each student or for each student group.

Procedure:

Note: This lesson may be presented during one or more class periods.

▸ Ask the students:

> ***Have you ever been angry at a friend or a sibling and said or done something that you later regretted?*** (As the students describe times when perhaps they were angry with a sibling or a friend and said or did things they later regretted, bring out the possibility that they regretted their actions not just because of the trouble they got into, but because after their anger was gone, they felt guilty.)

▸ Show the students the materials from the option that you chose. For instance—the paper plate and tube of toothpaste. Then say:

> ***Please raise your hands and share with us specific things that you or someone else has said or done that were disrespectful and/or mean.***

▶ As the students share specific words or actions, squeeze toothpaste onto the paper plate. Squeeze toothpaste out with each example. Continue as several students describe specific words and actions. If you are using the shaving cream, dispense some onto the plate with each example. Then say:

Now you are no longer angry and would like to take back all those hurtful, disrespectful things you said and did. I need a volunteer to come to the front of the classroom and help me put the toothpaste back into the tube/shaving cream back into the can.

▶ Choose a volunteer. When the volunteer comes to the front of the room, the volunteer and the rest of the students will realize that it is impossible to put the toothpaste back into the tube/shaving cream back into the can. Then say:

Boys and girls, please remember this activity when you get angry and want to say or do something disrespectful and hurtful. Once the words or actions are said or done, you cannot take them back.

▶ Have the students discuss the concept of not being able to take back any thing they said or did in anger.

▶ If time permits, you may begin the scenarios (pages 58-59) now or you may present the scenarios during a subsequent class period.

▶ Introduce the scenarios by saying:

Let's look at the role-plays and see if we can guide Alex and Maddie by using what we know about handling situations in which anger has been inappropriately displayed.

SCENARIO SUGGESTIONS:

1. Choose one or more scenarios. Read each chosen scenario to the students. Allow time for discussion after each scenario. Continue the discussion as long as the students offer choices and guidance for Maddie and Alex.

2. Divide the class into groups. Have each group role-play a different scenario illustrating choices based on good character traits. Allow time for discussion after each role-play.

3. Have the students read each scenario. After each scenario has been read, use the following questions to stimulate class discussion.

SUGGESTED SCENARIO DISCUSSION QUESTIONS:

Scenario #15

1. *What is the dilemma or problem that Alex is facing?* (Alex is getting angry with Maddie about the mess she leaves in the playroom.)

2. ***What are Alex's choices?*** (Alex can remember *The Golden Rule* and try to work out the disagreement with Maddie in a respectful and peaceful manner. He could hit Maddie. He could do nothing and continue to be angry.)

3. ***Have you ever been faced with a similar situation? What did you choose to say or do? Were you happy with your choice?*** (Accept all appropriate responses. Keep the students on the topic of not being able to take back things said or done in anger.)

4. ***What should Alex choose to say or do?*** (Alex should always remember *The Golden Rule* and try his best to work out the problem with Maddie. If the problem persists, Alex should ask his parents to sit down with him and help him come to a solution. Accept all other appropriate responses.)

Scenario #16

1. ***What is the problem or dilemma that Alex is facing?*** (Alex is facing several problems. Ben is angry. Alex is scared and angry because Ben has threatened him.)

2. ***What are Alex's choices?*** (Alex can remember *The Golden Rule* and try to handle the situation respectfully and peacefully. He can talk with an adult whom he trusts. He can do nothing. He can do exactly what Ben wants him to do.)

3. ***Have you ever been in a situation where you were threatened and became angry? How did you handle the situation? Do you feel that you made a good character choice in handling the situation?*** (Accept all appropriate responses. Keep the students on the topic of not being able to take back things said or done in anger.)

4. ***What should Alex choose to say or do?*** (Alex should calm down and do his best to handle this situation peacefully and respectfully. He may need to speak with his teacher, his principal, his parents, or an adult whom he trusts. Accept all other appropriate responses.)

Follow-Up Activities:

▸ Ask the students to conclude this lesson by summarizing its content and explaining how they would apply in their own lives what they have learned about *The Golden Rule*. (Accept all appropriate responses and guide the students in reflecting on *The Golden Rule*— Do unto others as you would have them do unto you. [Treat others as you would like to be treated.])

▸ Give each student paper and a pencil. Have the students write original scenarios based on *The Golden Rule*.

SCENARIO #15

Alex and Maddie share a playroom. This is a problem, because Maddie is sloppy. She throws her books, her clothes, her school supplies, her games, her toys, and other things everywhere. Alex and Maddie have had arguments over this situation. Their parents tell them to "work it out." When Alex tries to talk with Maddie, she won't listen. Alex is starting to get very angry about the situation.

What should Alex choose to say or do?

 ALEX & MADDIE: LIFE-SKILL LESSONS THROUGH ROLE-PLAY © 2006 MAR*CO PRODUCTS, INC. 1-800-448-2197

SCENARIO #16

Alex and Ben are in the bathroom at the same time. Ben was scolded by the teacher just before lunch. He is still angry about it. Ben tells Alex he hates this school and wants to trash it. Ben decides he wants to get paper towels, wet them, and throw them up onto the ceiling. He dares Alex to do it, too. Ben says that if Alex doesn't do it or if Alex tells on him, he will beat Alex up after school. Alex is scared and angry that Ben has threatened him.

What should Alex choose to say or do?

RESPECT: LESSON 3
MANNERS

Purpose:

The students will give examples of using good manners and polite language to show respect for others and role-play each example for the class. After reading or role-playing the scenarios, the students will have an opportunity to apply what they have learned by helping Alex and Maddie make decisions based on using good manners to show respect for others.

Materials Needed:

For the leader:
- ☐ Chart paper and marker
- ☐ Masking tape
- ☐ Scissors
- ☐ Container

For each student:
- ☐ Copy of *Scenario #17* (optional, page 63)
- ☐ Copy of *Scenario #18* (optional, page 64)
- ☐ Paper (optional)
- ☐ Pencil (optional)

Pre-Presentation Preparation:

Post the chart paper so you can write on it as the students cite examples of good manners and polite language.

Optional: Make a copy of the chosen scenarios for each student or for each student group.

Procedure:

Note: This lesson may be presented during one or more class periods.

▸ Introduce the lesson by saying:

> *Good manners show respect for others. Together, we're going to brainstorm a list of words and phrases that demonstrate good manners. I will write the words on the chart paper. When we have finished giving examples and writing them on the chart paper, I will cut out each word and have groups of two students choose an example and act out a situation in which that word or phrase could be used.*

Possible examples: *Please; thank you; yes, Ma'am; no, Ma'am; yes, Sir; no, Sir; excuse me,* etc. (You may want to group two of these together, in the interest of time.)

▸ As the students give suggestions, write them on the chart paper. Allow time for elaboration and discussion.

▸ When the students have finished making suggestions, cut out the phrases or words and fold the strips in half. Place the strips in a container.

▸ Divide the students into pairs and have each pair draw a strip of paper from the container.

▸ Allow approximately 10 minutes for the students to develop and practice their dialogues.

▸ Have the students perform their dialogues.

▸ If time permits, you may begin the scenarios (pages 63-64) now or you may present the scenarios during a subsequent class period.

▸ Introduce the scenarios by saying:

> ***Let's look at the role-plays and see if we can guide Alex and Maddie by using what we know about remembering to use good manners.***

SCENARIO SUGGESTIONS:

1. Choose one or more scenarios. Read each chosen scenario to the students. Allow time for discussion after each scenario. Continue the discussion as long as the students offer choices and guidance for Maddie and Alex.

2. Divide the class into groups. Have each group role-play a different scenario illustrating choices based on good character traits. Allow time for discussion after each role-play.

3. Have the students read each scenario. After each scenario has been read, use the following questions to stimulate class discussion.

SUGGESTED SCENARIO DISCUSSION QUESTIONS:

Scenario #17

1. ***What is the dilemma or problem that Alex is facing?*** (Alex is feeling uncomfortable using his good manners because few, if any, of the students in his class use them. On the other hand, his teacher, Mrs. Peyton, compliments Alex when he uses his good manners.)

2. **What are Alex's choices?** (Alex can quit using his good manners. He can continue using his good manners and not worry about how his classmates behave. He can discuss the situation with his parents.)

3. **Have you ever been embarrassed because you used good manners and someone made fun of you? What did you choose to do? Was that choice based on good character traits?** (Accept all appropriate responses. Keep the students on the topic of showing respect by displaying good manners toward adults.)

4. **What should Alex choose to say or do?** (Alex should continue to use his good manners and hope the other students learn from his example. Accept all other appropriate responses.)

Scenario #18

1. **What is the dilemma or problem that Maddie is facing?** (Maddie has been taught to respect her elders and knows that the other students' behavior does not display good manners and show respect. Does Maddie choose to act like her friends and push through the doors ahead of the teachers and other adults?)

2. **What are Maddie's choices?** (Maddie can forget what her parents have taught her about respecting her elders and act like her friends, pushing ahead of the teachers and other adults. Maddie can show her respect for teachers and other adults by using good manners and opening doors for them and letting them enter the building before she does.)

3. **Have you ever been faced with a similar situation? What did you choose to say or do? Were you happy with your choice?** (Accept all appropriate responses. Keep the students on the topic of showing respect by displaying good manners toward adults.)

4. **What should Maddie choose to say or do?** (Maddie should use her good manners to show respect for her elders by opening doors for them and letting them go through the doors before her. Maybe her friends will learn from her example. Accept all other appropriate responses.)

Follow-Up Activities:

▸ Revisit the students' definition of *respect*. You might what to add some specific mention of *manners* to this definition.

    Example: Remember to show particular respect to people who are older than you. One way to show respect is by using good manners.

▸ Give each student paper and a pencil. Have the students write original scenarios on showing *respect* by using good manners.

SCENARIO #17

Alex's parents have taught him to answer people very politely by saying *Yes, Sir; No, Sir; Excuse me; Please;* and *Thank you.* In Alex's class at school, no one ever uses these words. When Alex uses them in class, the other students look at him oddly. Alex wonders if they will start making fun of him and he can't decide if it would be best not to use such polite language. Alex's teacher, Mrs. Peyton, compliments Alex on his good manners. Alex feels very respectful and polite when he uses these words.

What should Alex choose to say or do?

SCENARIO #18

Maddie's parents have always emphasized that she and Alex must respect their elders (anyone older than them). One way that they do this is to always allow their elders to go through a door first and even hold the door open for the older person. Maddie has noticed that if a teacher or another adult is trying to get in or out of the school building after physical education class or after lunch, her friends just push ahead of the adults. At times, it almost seems as if the students push the elders out of the way. Maddie has been taught that this is not good manners and does not show respect for elders. She feels awkward pushing ahead of teachers and other adults, but wonders if she should act like her friends.

What should Maddie choose to say or do?

ALEX & MADDIE: LIFE-SKILL LESSONS THROUGH ROLE-PLAY © 2006 MAR*CO PRODUCTS, INC. 1-800-448-2197

TOLERANCE

Purpose:

The students will give their definition of *tolerance,* cite examples of ways that people display tolerant or intolerant behavior, and compare their definitions with the one in the dictionary. After reading or role-playing the scenarios, the students will apply their understanding of what tolerance is by helping Alex and Maddie make decisions based on good character traits.

Materials Needed:

For the leader:
- ☐ Chalkboard and chalk
- ☐ Chart paper and marker
- ☐ Dictionary (optional)

For each student:
- ☐ Copy of *Scenario #19* (optional, page 68)
- ☐ Copy of *Scenario #20* (optional, page 69)
- ☐ Paper (optional)
- ☐ Pencil (optional)

> ### DEFINITION OF
> ## Tolerance, Tolerant
>
> Tolerance: acceptance of beliefs, dress, and actions that are different from one's own
>
> Tolerant: willing to respect the beliefs of others

Pre-Presentation Preparation:

Write the words *tolerant* and *tolerance* on the chalkboard.

Optional: Make a copy of the chosen scenarios for each student or for each student group.

Procedure:

Note: This lesson may be presented during one or more class periods.

▸ Ask the students:

> **What do you think the words** tolerant **and** tolerance **mean?** (If they are having a difficult time with these words, give them a hint.)

Hint: Do you treat others well even if they look, dress, act, or believe differently than you?

- Have the students give examples of *tolerance* or *tolerant* behavior in their own lives. Cite an example of your own.

- Present the dictionary definitions or the definitions on page 65 of *tolerant* and *tolerance*. Then say:

    Our country is made up of many different cultures and of people who have emigrated from other countries. So the chances of seeing people who look, dress, act, or believe differently than we do is very good. We must learn to get along with everyone and be accepting of differences in others.

    Who can give us some examples of people we have seen who are different from us? (Accept all appropriate responses. Possible examples: Handicapped people, those who wear glasses, those who have braces, crippled people, blind people, those of nationalities other than our own, those who speak a foreign language, those who dress differently, etc.)

- If time permits, you may begin the scenarios (pages 68-69) now or you may present the scenarios during a subsequent class period.

- Introduce the scenarios by saying:

    Let's look at the role-plays and see if we can guide Alex and Maddie by using what we know about tolerant behavior.

SCENARIO SUGGESTIONS:

1. Choose one or more scenarios. Read each chosen scenario to the students. Allow time for discussion after each scenario. Continue the discussion as long as the students offer choices and guidance for Maddie and Alex.

2. Divide the class into groups. Have each group role-play a different scenario illustrating choices based on good character traits. Allow time for discussion after each role-play.

3. Have the students read each scenario. After each scenario has been read, use the following questions to stimulate class discussion.

SUGGESTED SCENARIO DISCUSSION QUESTIONS:

Scenario #19

1. ***What is the dilemma or problem that Alex is facing?*** (Alex can choose to make fun of the new students or not.)

2. ***What are Alex's choices?*** (Alex can be tolerant and accept that other people can look different, speak different languages, and dress differently. Alex can join the students

who are being disrespectful and make fun of the new students. Alex can speak with his parents or an adult whom he trusts.)

3. ***Have you ever faced a similar situation? What did you choose to do? Were you pleased with your decision?*** (Accept all appropriate responses. Keep the students on the topic of tolerance.)

4. ***What should Alex choose to say or do?*** (Alex should be tolerant and accept other people's differences. He should let his parents and/or an adult whom he trusts know that this treatment of the new students is taking place. Accept all other appropriate responses.)

Scenario #20

1. ***What is the dilemma or problem that Maddie is facing?*** (Maddie has to decide if she is willing to be disrespectful and intolerant of Veronica in order to keep Linda as a friend.)

2. ***How do you think Maddie feels about her friend Linda?*** (Accept all appropriate responses.)

3. ***What are Maddie's choices?*** (Maddie can listen to Linda and make fun of Veronica. Maddie can show tolerance and acceptance and be polite, friendly, and respectful to Veronica.)

4. ***Has this ever happened to you? How did you feel? What did you choose to do about it?*** (Accept all appropriate responses. Keep the students on the topic of showing tolerance.)

5. ***What should Maddie choose to say or do?*** (Maddie should be respectful and tolerant of Veronica's differences. She should be polite, friendly, and courteous to Veronica. She should also remember that the situation could be reversed and how she would feel if someone were intolerant and made fun of her differences. Accept all other appropriate responses.)

Follow-Up Activities:

▸ Revisit the class definition for *respect* and check to see if the students feel a need for revisions, additions, or changes. You may want to add some specific mention of *tolerance* to this definition.

   Example: It is okay for people to look different, speak different languages, or dress differently.

▸ Give each student paper and a pencil. Have the students write original scenarios on applying tolerance in their daily lives.

SCENARIO #19

A new family has moved into Alex's neighborhood. They are from a different country and wear clothes that reflect its culture. This is an unusual sight at Alex's school. At first, the students in Alex's classroom just stared at the new students. Now his classmates have decided that the way they dress is "uncool" and they make fun of the new students. Alex doesn't feel comfortable making fun of the new students, but he doesn't want his classmates to make fun of him, either. Would it be better for Alex to go along with the students in his classroom?

What should Alex choose to say or do?

ALEX & MADDIE: LIFE-SKILL LESSONS THROUGH ROLE-PLAY © 2006 MAR*CO PRODUCTS, INC. 1-800-448-2197

SCENARIO #20

A new girl named Veronica has just come into Maddie's classroom from another city. Veronica is very shy and she wears glasses. Maddie's friend, Linda, begins making fun of Veronica. In class, Linda quietly makes faces at Veronica when Veronica is not looking. Linda begins calling Veronica "Four Eyes" and wants Maddie to do the same. Maddie feels very uneasy about this, but she likes being Linda's friend. Maddie wonders how she would feel if she were the new girl in class and the situation were reversed.

What should Maddie choose to say or do?

RESPECT

_____

was caught showing
good character when
displaying *respect* by

_____

_____

_____

Date _____

Signature _____

ALEX & MADDIE: LIFE-SKILL LESSONS THROUGH ROLE-PLAY © 2006 MAR+CO PRODUCTS, INC. 1-800-448-2197

RESPONSIBLITY

Topic Objectives:

To help children realize the value of:

Always trying to do their best.

Remembering to think before they act and that actions have consequences.

Not giving up—continuing to try.

Doing something they are supposed to do.

Using self-discipline and self-control.

INTRODUCTION

Purpose:

To help students understand the meaning of *responsibility*

Materials Needed:

For the leader:
- ☐ Chart paper and marker
- ☐ Masking tape
- ☐ Dictionary (optional)

For each student:
None

Pre-Presentation Preparation:

None

DEFINITION OF
Responsible, Responsibility

Responsible: being held accountable, ability to know right from wrong, attending to obligations and duties

Responsibility: the act of being responsible

Procedure:

▸ Introduce the topic by having the students define, in their own words, what *responsibility* means to them. Guide the students to a definition.

> Possible examples: A person shows responsibility by doing what he/she is supposed to do. A person is responsible if he/she can be counted on to try to do the right thing.

▸ After the students have agreed on a class definition of *responsibility*, write the definition on chart paper and post the paper in a place in the classroom where everyone can see it for future reference. The students may want to revise or add to the definition as the lessons on responsibility progress. You may give them the definition found above or the dictionary definition. Compare their definition to the formal definition. Make any changes the students or you believe are necessary at this time.

ACTIONS HAVE GOOD OR BAD CONSEQUENCES

Purpose:

The students will learn that all actions have either positive or negative consequences. After reading or role-playing the scenarios, the students will apply this knowledge to help guide Alex and Maddie through several situations.

Materials Needed:

For the leader:
- ☐ Chart paper and marker
- ☐ Masking tape

For each student:
- ☐ Copy of *Scenario #21* (optional, page 77)
- ☐ Copy of *Scenario #22* (optional, page 78)
- ☐ Copy of *Scenario #23* (optional, page 79)
- ☐ Paper (optional)
- ☐ Pencil (optional)

Pre-Presentation Preparation:

Divide the chart paper into two columns. Label the columns *Good Choices* and *Poor Choices*. Then hang the paper in the room where all of the students can see it.

Optional: Make a copy of the chosen scenarios for each student or for each student group.

Procedure:

Note: This lesson may be presented during one or more class periods.

▸ Begin by asking the students:

> **Have you ever made decisions?** (Accept all appropriate responses.)

> **Were the consequences of your decisions positive or negative?** (Accept all appropriate responses.)

▸ Then say:

> *Let's make a list of actions or decisions and decide if each was a good choice or a poor choice. Good choices result in positive consequences. Poor choices result in negative consequences. As you suggest the actions or decisions, we will decide as a class if they should be listed under* Good Choices *or* Poor Choices.

▸ Have the students name actions or decisions. Then discuss with the class under which heading each should be listed. Write the choices in the appropriate columns on the chart paper.

Examples that the students might give are:

- Take your classmate's glue without asking. (Poor Choice)
- Call your friends disrespectful names. (Poor Choice)
- Cross the street without looking both ways. (Poor Choice)
- Hit your little brother or sister on purpose. (Poor Choice)
- Tell your teacher that she dropped some money on the way to lunch. (Good Choice)
- Work hard every day in class. (Good Choice)
- Study hard before a test. (Good Choice)

▸ Leave the *Good Choices/Poor Choices* chart hanging in the classroom. You and the students may want to add to it during a future lesson.

▸ Say to the students:

> *As you can see, our actions have either positive or negative consequences. I prefer positive consequences. Which type of consequences would make you feel better?* (Accept all appropriate responses, being sure to keep the students on task.)

▸ If time permits, you may begin the scenarios (pages 77-79) now or you may present the scenarios during a subsequent class period.

▸ Introduce the scenarios by saying:

> *Let's look at the role-plays and see if we can guide Alex and Maddie by using what we know about positive and negative consequences.*

SCENARIO SUGGESTIONS:

1. Choose one or more scenarios. Read each chosen scenario to the students. Allow time for discussion after each scenario. Continue the discussion as long as the students offer choices and guidance for Maddie and Alex.

2. Divide the class into groups. Have each group role-play a different scenario illustrating choices based on good character traits. Allow time for discussion after each role-play.

3. Have the students read each scenario. After each scenario has been read, use the following questions to stimulate class discussion.

SUGGESTED SCENARIO DISCUSSION QUESTIONS:

Scenario #21

1. *What is the dilemma or problem that Maddie is facing?* (Maddie wants to impress George and needs to decide if she will do something she knows is wrong to help him solve his problem.)

2. *What are Maddie's choices?* (Maddie can slip George her book once her teacher has checked her textbooks. Maddie can simply say, "No, I'm sorry." Maddie can tell George to just tell the truth.)

3. *Has a friend ever asked you to do something that you knew was wrong? What choice did you make? Was it a responsible one?* (Accept all appropriate responses. Keep the students on the topic that choices/actions have consequences.)

4. *What should Maddie choose to say or do?* (Maddie needs to remember that all her actions/choices have consequences. She needs to say, "No, I'm sorry." If she chooses to allow George to use her book and say that it is his, she is helping him lie. It would be better for everyone if George were responsible and just told the truth. Accept all other appropriate responses.)

Scenario #22

1. *What is the dilemma or problem that Alex is facing?* (Alex must decide if he is responsible or if he will be persuaded by others to do something wrong.)

2. *What are Alex's choices?* (Alex can choose to be responsible, accept his role as class leader, and guide the substitute teacher as best he can. Alex can choose to be irresponsible and go along with those asking him to deceive the substitute teacher and cause problems.)

3. *Have you ever been in a similar situation, torn between making a responsible choice or not? What did you choose to do? Was it a responsible decision?* (Accept all appropriate responses. Keep the students on the topic of responsible choices.)

4. *What should Alex choose to say or do?* (Alex should remember that making an irresponsible choice will have only negative consequences. He should be a responsible class leader and help the substitute teacher as best he can. Accept all other appropriate responses.)

1. ***What is the dilemma or problem that Alex is facing?*** (Alex must decide what to do with what he knows about the gun Nathan has brought to school.)

2. ***What are Alex's choices?*** (Alex can do nothing. He can talk with an adult at school whom he trusts. He can tell Nathan to ask for help.)

3. ***Have you ever been in a similar situation? What did you choose to do? Was it a good choice?*** (Accept all appropriate responses. Keep the students on the topic of responsible decision-making and reinforce the concept that all actions have consequences.)

4. ***What should Alex choose to say or do?*** (Alex should immediately speak with an adult at school whom he trusts. Accept all other appropriate responses.)

Follow-Up Activities:

▸ Give each student paper and a pencil. Have the students write about three major choices they must make each day. Have the students share their choices with the class.

▸ Give each student paper and a pencil. Have the students write original scenarios emphasizing that actions have consequences—positive or negative.

SCENARIO #21

It is the end of the grading period at school. Mrs. Wheeler, Maddie's teacher, always does a book check at this time to make sure that all the books are accounted for. George forgot his math book today and asked Maddie to slip him her book once Mrs. Wheeler had checked all of Maddie's textbooks. George is a good guy and kind of cute, too.

What should Maddie choose to say or do?

SCENARIO #22

Each week, the teacher selects a different student to be class leader. Alex is leader for his classroom this week. Mr. Tonsing, Alex's teacher, is absent on Wednesday. One of the duties of the class leader is to help the substitute teacher with any questions he/she might have. Some of Alex's buddies suggest that he give the substitute the wrong information so that the class routine is not followed. These same students even want Alex to tell the substitute that on Wednesdays, Mr. Tonsing does not assign homework.

What should Alex choose to say or do?

 ALEX & MADDIE: LIFE-SKILL LESSONS THROUGH ROLE-PLAY © 2006 MAR*CO PRODUCTS, INC. 1-800-448-2197

SCENARIO #23

Nathan came to school today wearing a jacket. This seems odd to the rest of the boys in Alex's class, because it is a warm spring day. At recess, Nathan shows the boys a gun he has brought from home. He is wearing the jacket to conceal the gun, which is in a pocket. He brought the gun because he is trying to get out of a gang and is afraid that the gang members will beat him up after school. Nathan asked the boys not to tell anyone about the gun.

What should Alex choose to say or do?

RESPONSIBILITY: LESSON 2
JUST DO IT! AND DO YOUR BEST!

Purpose:

The students will discuss the importance of being *responsible* and doing what is expected of them even when they would rather not. The students will also discuss the importance of doing their best in everything they do. After reading or role-playing the scenarios, the students will apply their understanding of the lesson by guiding Alex and Maddie through several situations.

Materials Needed:

For the leader:
   None

For each student:
- ☐ Lined sheet of notebook paper
- ☐ Pencil
- ☐ Copy of *Scenario #24* (optional, page 84)
- ☐ Copy of *Scenario #25* (optional, page 85)
- ☐ Copy of *Scenario #26* (optional, page 86)
- ☐ Copy of *Scenario #27* (optional, page 87)
- ☐ Drawing paper for lower grades (optional)
- ☐ Crayons or markers for lower grades (optional)
- ☐ Paper (optional)
- ☐ Pencil (optional)

Pre-Presentation Preparation:

Optional: Make a copy of the chosen scenarios for each student or for each student group.

Procedure:

Note: This lesson may be presented during one or more class periods.

▸ Have the students pull out a sheet of paper and a pencil or distribute a sheet of lined paper and a pencil to each student. Then say:

    1. **Write My Responsibilities** *at the top of your paper.*

80 *ALEX & MADDIE: LIFE-SKILL LESSONS THROUGH ROLE-PLAY* © 2006 MAR✶CO PRODUCTS, INC. 1-800-448-2197

2. *Fold your sheet of paper in half lengthwise. In the upper-left hand column, write* At Home. *In the upper-right hand column, write* At School.

3. *In the appropriate columns, list your top three responsibilities at home and at school.*

▸ Give the students approximately 5-10 minutes, depending on grade level, to make their lists. When they have finished, have them share their responsibilities with the class. Allow time for discussion of the students' responsibilities.

▸ Ask the students:

What would happen if you chose not to fulfill your responsibilities or if you chose to not perform your responsibilities to the best of your ability? (Accept all appropriate responses. Keep the students on the topic of being responsible, doing what is expected of them, and doing it to the best of their ability.)

What makes you feel better—when you just barely get by with little effort or when you do what you need to do, even if you would rather not, and do it well? (Accept all appropriate responses.)

▸ If time permits, you may begin the scenarios (pages 84-87) now or you may present the scenarios during a subsequent class period.

▸ Introduce the scenarios by saying:

Let's look at the role-plays and see if we can guide Alex and Maddie by using what we know about the importance of being responsible.

SCENARIO SUGGESTIONS:

1. Choose one or more scenarios. Read each chosen scenario to the students. Allow time for discussion after each scenario. Continue the discussion as long as the students offer choices and guidance for Maddie and Alex.

2. Divide the class into groups. Have each group role-play a different scenario illustrating choices based on good character traits. Allow time for discussion after each role-play.

3. Have the students read each scenario. After each scenario has been read, use the following questions to stimulate class discussion.

SUGGESTED SCENARIO DISCUSSION QUESTIONS:

Scenario #24

1. *What is the situation that Maddie is facing?* (Maddie does not want to wash dishes tonight. She scraped her finger at school today.)

2. *What are Maddie's choices?* (Maddie can choose to whine about her cut finger and elicit sympathy from her parents who, hopefully, will ask Alex to wash dishes for her. Maddie can realize that she is merely trying to get out of doing her chores by exaggerating the cut on her finger. If Maddie's finger is really seriously cut, she can offer to trade days with Alex.)

3. *Have you ever tried to get out of doing a chore? How did you handle it? Do you feel that you made a choice based on good character traits?* (Accept all appropriate responses. Keep students on the topic of being responsible and doing what needs to be done even if they might not feel like it.)

4. *What should Maddie choose to say or do?* (Maddie should first decide if her finger is really too deeply cut to wash the dishes. If it is not, she should wash the dishes. She can show her finger to her mother. If Maddie's mother feels her finger is deeply cut, perhaps she can trade nights with Alex. Accept all other appropriate responses.)

Scenario #25

1. *What is the problem or dilemma that Maddie is facing?* (Alex is starting to forget his responsibility to Annie and his agreement with his parents. A big problem is that Alex gets angry when Maddie reminds him of his responsibility.)

2. *What are Maddie's choices?* (Maddie can let Annie go without food and water when it is Alex's day to take care of the dog. Maddie can just feed Annie for Alex and give her water when he forgets. Maddie can try talking with Alex one more time. Maddie can sit down with Mom and Dad and discuss the problem.)

3. *Has a similar situation ever happened to you? How did you choose to handle the situation? Did you make a good decision?* (Accept all appropriate responses. Keep the students on the topic of responsibility and the consequences that occur when we do not fulfill our responsibilities. Example: Annie could get sick from lack of food and water.)

4. *What should Maddie choose to say or do?* (Maddie should talk with Alex one more time. If that does not work, she needs to talk with Mom and Dad and explain the situation. Accept all other appropriate responses.)

Scenario #26

1. *What is the problem or dilemma that Alex is facing?* (Alex did not study and received a poor test grade.)

2. *What are Alex's choices?* (Alex can make excuses for his poor grade. He can blame the teacher. He can "fess up" and take responsibility by admitting that he did not study as much as he should have.)

3. ***Have you ever made a low test grade and been tempted to make excuses for it? What did you tell your parents and yourself? Was your decision a responsible one and did you admit your mistake?*** (Accept all appropriate responses. Keep the students on the topic of doing their best and accepting the consequences of making poor choices.)

4. ***What should Alex choose to say or do?*** (Alex should take full responsibility for not performing well on the test because he did not study as he should have. He should also learn from his mistake and be responsible next time. Accept all other appropriate responses.)

Scenario #27

1. ***What is the problem or dilemma that Alex is facing?*** (Alex has to decide how much effort to put forth on the assignment.)

2. ***What are Alex's choices?*** (Alex can choose to put out just enough effort to get a passing grade. Alex can work up to his potential and earn a high grade.)

3. ***Can you remember a time when you were in a similar situation? What did you finally choose to do? Was that a responsible choice?*** (Accept all appropriate responses. Keep the students on the topic of doing their best.)

4. ***What should Alex choose to say or do?*** (Alex should be responsible, work up to his potential, and strive to get as good a grade as possible. Accept all other appropriate responses.)

Follow-Up Activities:

▸ Ask the students:

   How do you feel when you do a job/assignment/chore and you know that you have worked to the very best of your ability? (Allow the students to respond. Emphasize that a job well done makes us feel good about ourselves and our pride shows in all of our work.)

▸ Give each student paper and a pencil. Have the students write original scenarios emphasizing the importance of doing what is expected of them and doing it to the best of their ability.

▸ Lower-grade students: Give each student drawing paper and crayons or markers. Have the students draw pictures of themselves doing their chores and doing them very well.

SCENARIO #24

Alex and Maddie take turns washing dishes after dinner. It is not Maddie's favorite thing to do. Today in gym class, Maddie cut her finger. Maddie knows that if she whines enough, her parents will ask Alex to take her turn at washing the dishes tonight. All she has to do is whine.

What should Maddie choose to say or do?

 ALEX & MADDIE: LIFE-SKILL LESSONS THROUGH ROLE-PLAY © 2006 MAR✱CO PRODUCTS, INC. 1-800-448-2197

SCENARIO #25

Alex and Maddie have always wanted a pet dog. They have asked their mom and dad many times to let them have one. Finally, their parents agree that they may have a dog if they are completely responsible for feeding it, keeping its water bowl full, and bathing and exercising their pet. For the first month or two, both Alex and Maddie were very responsible. Lately, Alex has begun to forget to feed Annie, their new dog. When Maddie reminds Alex, he gets angry with her.

What should Maddie choose to say or do?

SCENARIO #26

Alex had a big test in class the other day. He studied, but he knew he hadn't studied as much as he should have. His two favorite TV shows were on the night before the test and he watched them instead of studying. When he took the test, it seemed difficult. The teacher returned Alex's graded test today. Alex is horrified with the grade. To make matters worse, he has to take the test home and have his parents sign it. Alex's first instinct is to make excuses and blame the teacher for making the test so hard.

What should Alex choose to say or do?

 ALEX & MADDIE: LIFE-SKILL LESSONS THROUGH ROLE-PLAY © 2006 MAR*CO PRODUCTS, INC. 1-800-448-2197

SCENARIO #27

Alex is a smart young man and schoolwork has always been easy for him. It seems that he grasps concepts easily and manages to finish his projects and assignments very quickly. Mrs. Ray has given an assignment Alex can finish very quickly with little effort and do an okay job. On the other hand, Alex could really take his time, put a lot of effort into the assignment, and do an outstanding job.

What should Alex choose to say or do?

SELF-DISCIPLINE/SELF-CONTROL

Purpose:

The students will analyze different situations and determine how to add self-control or self-discipline to the situation. After reading or role-playing the scenarios, the students will apply what they have learned to guide Alex and Maddie through several situations.

Materials Needed:

For the leader:
- ☐ Copy of *Lower-Elementary Situations* (page 91)
- ☐ Copy of *Upper-Elementary Situations* (page 92)
- ☐ Scissors
- ☐ Container

For each student:
- ☐ Copy of *Scenario #28* (optional, page 93)
- ☐ Copy of *Scenario #29* (optional, page 94)
- ☐ Paper (optional)
- ☐ Pencil (optional)
- ☐ Drawing paper for lower grades (optional)
- ☐ Crayons or markers for lower grades (optional)

Pre-Presentation Preparation:

Make a copy of the *Upper-Elementary Situations* or *Lower-Elementary Situations*. Cut the situations apart. Place the slips of paper in a container.

Optional: Make a copy of the chosen scenarios for each student or for each student group.

Procedure:

Note: This lesson may be presented during one or more class periods.

▸ Lead a discussion on the meaning of *self-discipline* and *self-control*. Make sure the students have a clear understanding of both terms. (Self-control is having control over your actions and feelings. Self-discipline is the trait you use in order to exercise self-control.)

▸ Say to the students:

Today we are going to talk about times when we need to really think about our choices and add some self-control and self-discipline to our choices before we make matters worse.

I am going to ask for a volunteer to draw a slip of paper out of this container. Then, as a group, we will discuss how to best handle the situation, adding self-control and self-discipline to our choice.

▸ Select a student to pull a slip of paper out of the container. Read the situation described on the paper aloud, then have the students discuss what they believe are the best ways to handle the situation. Remember to keep the students focused on the importance of thinking before they act and the importance of self-discipline and self-control. Continue the activity as long as time permits or the students remain interested.

▸ If time permits, you may begin the scenarios (pages 93-94) now or you may present the scenarios during a subsequent class period.

▸ Introduce the scenarios by saying:

Let's look at the role-plays and see if we can guide Alex and Maddie by using what we know about using self-discipline and self-control when making choices.

SCENARIO SUGGESTIONS:

1. Choose one or more scenarios. Read each chosen scenario to the students. Allow time for discussion after each scenario. Continue the discussion as long as the students offer choices and guidance for Maddie and Alex.

2. Divide the class into groups. Have each group role-play a different scenario illustrating choices based on good character traits. Allow time for discussion after each role-play.

3. Have the students read each scenario. After each scenario has been read, use the following questions to stimulate class discussion.

SUGGESTED SCENARIO DISCUSSION QUESTIONS:

Scenario #28

1. *What is the dilemma or problem that Alex is facing?* (Alex is being tempted to do something illegal.)

2. *What are Alex's choices?* (Alex can say *no* and walk away. Alex can accept the offer. Alex can say *no*, walk away, and tell his parents about the incident.)

3. ***Have you ever been offered something that you know it would be wrong to accept? What did you do? Was it a responsible choice?*** (Accept all appropriate responses. Keep the students on the topic of having self-control and self-discipline.)

4. ***What should Alex choose to say or do?*** (Alex should say *no*, walk away, and discuss the incident with his parents or other adults whom he trusts. Accept all other appropriate responses.)

Scenario #29

1. ***What is the situation that Maddie is facing?*** (Whether to play with real guns.)

2. ***What are Maddie's choices?*** (Maddie can choose to say *no* and go home. Maddie can play with the real guns. Maddie can tell Jessica that she thinks playing with guns is a really bad idea. Maddie can talk with her parents about this incident.)

3. ***Have you ever been in a similar situation? What did you choose to do? Was your choice a responsible decision?*** (Accept all appropriate responses. Keep the students on the topic of self-discipline and self-control.)

4. ***What should Maddie choose to say or do?*** (Maddie should tell Jessica that this is a really bad idea, and say *no* to playing with the guns. Maddie should also go home and discuss the incident with her parents. Jessica's parents need to know that she is handling those guns. Accept all other appropriate responses.)

Follow-Up Activities:

▸ Revisit the class definition for *responsibility* and check to see if the students feel a need for revisions, additions, or changes.

▸ Give each student paper and a pencil. Have the students write original scenarios in which they show that self-discipline and self-control are important elements of being responsible. If there is enough time, have the students share their scenarios with the class.

▸ Lower-grade students: Give each student drawing paper and crayons or markers. Have the students draw pictures of themselves using self control. When everyone has finished drawing, allow time for sharing.

▸ Have a student summarize the underlying theme of the lesson. (The students should speak to the importance of thinking before we say or do something we might regret later. The students should also emphasize the importance of self-control and self-discipline in our daily lives.)

LOWER-ELEMENTARY SITUATIONS

(You may add any other situations that may be more relevant for your students.)

You do not like the lesson and feel like scribbling all over the top of your desk.

Another student does something to upset you and you feel like kicking him.

You are angry at your mom and dad and you feel like kicking your pet or pulling its tail.

Your little sister has been touching your things without your permission and you feel like pinching her.

You are noticing things that the other students do and want to tell the teacher (tattle) about them.

A classmate has brought a pocketknife to school and is showing everyone how well it cuts. You are tempted to play with it.

You brought some Halloween candy to school and it is in your desk. You feel like eating some during the lesson.

UPPER-ELEMENTARY SITUATIONS

(You may add any other situations that may be more relevant for your students.)

You think about e-mailing your friends nasty remarks about a teacher who made you angry today.

You are tempted to skip school today and go to the movies or to the mall with a friend.

Your friend invites you to the movies, but you have spent all your allowance for the week. You think how easy it would be to take money from your mother's wallet without her knowing.

A lower-grade student on the monkey bars is going very slowly and you think about pushing her out of the way.

At recess, your friends forget to bring the ball and you think how easy it would be to snatch a ball away from a younger student.

A classmate brought cigarettes to school and wants to share one with you after school.

You feel like hitting your younger brother for touching your things without your permission.

 ALEX & MADDIE: LIFE-SKILL LESSONS THROUGH ROLE-PLAY © 2006 MAR*CO PRODUCTS, INC. 1-800-448-2197

SCENARIO #28

While Alex is shopping at the local mall, he meets a group of older boys from his school. Two of the boys offer Alex drugs.

What should Alex choose to say or do?

SCENARIO #29

Maddie is playing at her friend Jessica's house while Jessica's parents are not at home. Jessica shows Maddie where her dad hides his guns. Jessica takes two of the guns out and says that she and Maddie can use them to pretend that they are secret agents.

What should Maddie choose to say or do?

 ALEX & MADDIE: LIFE-SKILL LESSONS THROUGH ROLE-PLAY © 2006 MAR✶CO PRODUCTS, INC. 1-800-448-2197

RESPONSIBILITY

_____

was caught showing
good character when
displaying *responsibility* by

_____

_____

_____

Date _____

Signature _____

FAIRNESS

Topic Objectives:

To help children realize the value of:

Sharing and taking turns.

Listening to others and being open-minded.

Following the rules in everything they do.

Not blaming others if things don't work out.

Making sure not to take advantage of others or of their trust.

FAIRNESS
INTRODUCTION

Purpose:

To help students understand the meaning of *fairness*

Materials Needed:

For the leader:
- ☐ Chart paper and marker
- ☐ Masking tape
- ☐ Dictionary (optional)

For each student:
None

Pre-Presentation Preparation:

None

Procedure:

▸ Introduce the topic by having the students define, in their own words, what *fair* means to them. Guide the students to a definition.

> Possible examples: A fair person plays by the rules. A fair person doesn't cheat. A person who is fair treats everyone equally.

▸ After the students have agreed on a class definition of *fair*, write the definition on chart paper and post the paper in a place in the classroom where everyone can see it for future reference. The students may want to revise or add to the definition as the lessons on fairness progress. You may give them the definition found above or the dictionary definition. Compare their definition to the formal definition. Make any changes the students or you believe are necessary at this time.

DEFINITION OF
Fair, Fairness

Fair: playing according to the rules, observing the rules. Someone who is fair is characterized by honesty.

Fairness: the quality of being fair

FOLLOW THE RULES

Purpose:

The students will discuss where rules are found in their daily lives and the importance of these rules. They will come up with a name, logo, and rules for their cooperative groups that promote fair behavior. After reading or role-playing the scenarios, the students will apply their knowledge of fairness by helping Alex and Maddie make decisions based on the character trait of *following the rules*.

Materials Needed:

For the leader:
- ☐ Timer
- ☐ Masking tape

For each student:
- ☐ Copy of *Scenario #30* (optional, page 104)
- ☐ Copy of *Scenario #31* (optional, page 105)
- ☐ Copy of *Scenario #32* (optional, page 106)
- ☐ Copy of *Scenario #33* (optional, page 107)
- ☐ Copy of *Scenario #34* (optional, page 108)
- ☐ Paper (optional)
- ☐ Pencil (optional)

For each student group:
- ☐ Chart paper
- ☐ Markers or crayons

Pre-Presentation Preparation:

Optional: Make a copy of the chosen scenarios for each student or for each student group.

Procedure:

Note: This lesson may be presented during one or more class periods.

▶ Introduce the lesson by asking:

Boys and girls, what are rules? (_Rules_ are directions/guidelines that we have to follow to keep our classroom, homes, streets, etc. in order. Accept all appropriate responses.)

Where do we find rules? (We find rules on playing fields, in schools, in cities, on streets, in courts, coming and going between countries, etc. Accept all appropriate responses.)

Are rules good or bad? (Rules are good for society and for us. They keep things running smoothly and in an orderly way. Accept all appropriate responses.)

▶ Then say:

Today I will divide you into cooperative groups. Each group will develop rules for your cooperative team. Each group will come up with a team name, team logo, and team rules that promote fairness.

▶ Divide the students into groups of three or four. Distribute chart paper and markers/crayons to each group. Then say:

You will have 10-20 (determine the amount of minutes based on the grade level) **_minutes to develop your team logo, team name, and team rules that promote fairness. I will set the timer for_** (however many minutes you have given them) **_and we will share our ideas when the timer goes off._**

▶ When time is called, have the groups share their team names, team logos, and team rules. Compare them. Post the team rules, names, and logos near each team. As teams work cooperatively, these may be used to remind the students to "follow the team rules."

▶ If time permits, you may begin the scenarios (pages 104-108) now or you may present the scenarios during a subsequent class period.

▶ Introduce the scenarios by saying:

Let's look at the role-plays and see if we can guide Alex and Maddie by using what we know about reacting to situations in a fair manner.

SCENARIO SUGGESTIONS:

1. Choose one or more scenarios. Read each chosen scenario to the students. Allow time for discussion after each scenario. Continue the discussion as long as the students offer choices and guidance for Maddie and Alex.

2. Divide the class into groups. Have each group role-play a different scenario illustrating choices based on good character traits. Allow time for discussion after each role-play.

3. Have the students read each scenario. After each scenario has been read, use the following questions to stimulate class discussion.

SUGGESTED SCENARIO DISCUSSION QUESTIONS:

Scenario #30

1. *What is the dilemma or problem that Maddie is facing?* (Maddie did not tag Veronica out, but the rest of the team thinks she did.)

2. *What are Maddie's choices?* (Maddie can be fair and admit that she did not tag Veronica out. Maddie can act like she did tag her out, since the rest of the team thinks Maddie was successful. Maddie can let the teams argue about it and see what happens.)

3. *Besides fairness, what other character trait is involved in Maddie's decision?* (The other trait involved is *honesty* or *trustworthiness*. Accept all appropriate responses.)

4. *Have you ever been faced with a similar situation? How did you handle it? How do you feel about the decision you made?* (Accept all appropriate responses. Keep the students on the topic of fairness and following the rules.)

5. *What should Maddie choose to say or do?* (Maddie should be fair, honest, and follow the rules and admit that she did not tag Veronica out. Accept all other appropriate responses.)

Scenario #31

1. *What is the dilemma or problem that Maddie is facing?* (Maddie is hungry and does not want to get at the end of the line and wait her turn.)

2. *What are Maddie's choices?* (Maddie can take the "cuts in line" that Mary is offering her. Maddie can be fair and follow the rules and just get at the end of the line.)

3. *What have you done in similar situations? Was it the fair thing to do?* (Accept all appropriate responses. Keep the students on the topic of fairness and following the rules.)

4. *What should Maddie choose to say or do?* (Maddie should get at the end of the line. Accept all other appropriate responses.)

Scenario #32

1. *What is the dilemma or problem that Alex is facing?* (Alex has just seen Jon erase Tiffanye's name and write his own on her test paper.)

2. *What are Alex's choices?* (Alex can ignore what he saw and act like nothing happened. After all, it does not affect him. Alex can tell Jon what he saw. Alex can tell Tiffanye. Alex can tell the teacher when he gives her the test papers.)

3. *What other character trait is involved in this role-play?* (Alex must show responsibility and let someone in authority know when he sees someone do something that is wrong. Jon is not being honest or trustworthy.)

4. *Can you remember a time that you were faced with a similar situation? What did you choose to do? Do you feel that your choice was a fair one?* (Accept all appropriate responses. Keep the students on the topic of following the rules and fairness.)

5. *What should Alex choose to say or do?* (Alex should tell the teacher what he just witnessed. Accept all other appropriate responses.)

Scenario #33

1. *What is the situation or dilemma that Alex is facing?* (Alex's teammates begin not following the rules of soccer and begin tripping players on the opposing team.)

2. *What are Alex's choices?* (Alex can join in tripping the players on the other team. Alex can tell his teammates that winning is no fun when you don't follow the rules.)

3. *Have you ever been in a similar situation? How did you choose to handle the situation? Were you pleased with your decision?* (Accept all appropriate responses and keep the students on the topic of following the rules and fair play.)

4. *What should Alex choose to say or do?* (Alex should tell his teammates that winning is no fun when you don't follow the rules. He should definitely not join in tripping the other team's players. He should play by the rules and play fair. Accept all other appropriate responses.)

Scenario #34

1. *What is the dilemma or problem that Alex is facing?* (Alex's soccer coach is teaching the team to cheat, to not play fair, and to not play by the rules.)

2. *What are Alex's choices?* (Alex can do nothing and learn how to cheat. Alex can talk with his parents or other adults whom he trusts and ask for direction and help.)

3. *Have you ever had a coach or teacher encourage you to cheat? How did you feel? How did you handle the situation? Were you happy with your decision?* (Accept all appropriate responses. Keep the students on the topic of following the rules and playing fair.)

4. ***What should Alex choose to say or do?*** (Alex should definitely talk with his parents or other adults whom he trusts and get direction and help. Alex knows that not following the rules is wrong and he does not have to be a part of it. Accept all other appropriate responses.)

Follow-Up Activities:

▶ Ask the students:

> ***Why are rules important?*** (Rules keep our lives running in an orderly fashion. Accept all appropriate responses.)

▶ Then say:

> ***When you are tempted to not follow the rules, ask yourself, "Would it be good if all people chose not to follow this rule?" Your answer would probably be "NO!"***

▶ Give each student paper and a pencil. Have the students write original scenarios on the topic of *following rules*.

SCENARIO #30

At recess today, Maddie's class is playing kickball. Veronica kicks the ball a long way and is running from second to third base. Maddie receives the ball from the outfield and tries to tag Veronica out, but misses. However, the rest of the team seems to think that Maddie did tag Veronica out.

What should Maddie choose to say or do?

 ALEX & MADDIE: LIFE-SKILL LESSONS THROUGH ROLE-PLAY © 2006 MAR∗CO PRODUCTS, INC. 1-800-448-2197

SCENARIO #31

On the way to the cafeteria at lunchtime, Maddie stops at the restroom. When she gets to the cafeteria, the line is very long. One of her friends, Mary, motions to Maddie to come ahead and Mary will give Maddie "cuts" in line. Maddie is hungry and does not want to wait in line.

What should Maddie choose to say or do?

SCENARIO #32

As Alex is collecting spelling tests, he sees Jon erase Tiffanye's name and write his own name on Tiffanye's test paper. Tiffanye always gets good scores on her spelling tests. This will not affect Alex at all, but is it fair to Tiffanye?

What should Alex choose to say or do?

 ALEX & MADDIE: LIFE-SKILL LESSONS THROUGH ROLE-PLAY © 2006 MAR*CO PRODUCTS, INC. 1-800-448-2197

SCENARIO #33

At recess today, Coach Barker divides the class into six teams to play soccer on three different fields. Everyone is having a good time until a player on Alex's team decides to start tripping the players on the other team. Some of the students are getting hurt. Coach Barker is helping other teams across the field and is not aware of what is happening.

What should Alex choose to say or do?

SCENARIO #34

Alex plays on a soccer team after school and on weekends. His coach, Mr. Setnom, loves to win games any way he can. Today at practice, he is teaching Alex and his teammates how to pull the opposing players' shirts to hold them back while running during a game. Mr. Setnom says he will teach them to do this so the referee will not see them do it during the game.

What should Alex choose to say or do?

ALEX & MADDIE: LIFE-SKILL LESSONS THROUGH ROLE-PLAY © 2006 MAR∗CO PRODUCTS, INC. 1-800-448-2197

BE SURE TO NOT TAKE ADVANTAGE OF OTHERS OR OF THEIR TRUST

Purpose:

The students will discuss their feelings about the teacher's unfairness during the lesson. After reading or role-playing the scenarios, the students will apply what they have learned about being fair to guide Alex and Maddie through several situations.

Materials Needed:

For the leader:
- ☐ Stickers, small pieces of candy, pencils, coupons (something small that you can give each student)

For each student:
- ☐ Copy of *Scenario #35* (optional, page 113)
- ☐ Copy of *Scenario #36* (optional, page 114)
- ☐ Copy of *Scenario #37* (optional, page 115)
- ☐ Copy of *Scenario #38* (optional, page 116)
- ☐ Paper (optional)
- ☐ Pencil (optional)

Pre-Presentation Preparation:

Optional: Make a copy of the chosen scenarios for each student or for each student group.

Procedure:

Note: This lesson may be presented during one or more class periods.

▸ Distribute one of the items mentioned in the *Materials Needed* leader's section to each student. Then say:

> *My birthday is in* _____. *How many of you were also born in* _____? (Pause for student responses.) *Isn't that a great month?*

▸ Give each of those students born in your birthday month an extra of whatever you have distributed to the entire class.

▸ You will probably hear some grumbling. Then ask:

What just happened here? What did I just do? (You gave an extra_____ to those students born in the same month as you. You were unfair. You have favorites. Accept all appropriate responses.)

How did my behavior make you feel? (Those getting only one item might say: I felt left out. I felt that you didn't like me. I was hurt. I felt you were unfair. I didn't like you. Accept all appropriate responses. Those getting more than one item might say: I liked it. I felt that you liked me more than the students not born in your birthday month. I liked you. Accept all appropriate responses.)

Did I abuse my power as a teacher? Was I being fair? (You did take advantage of being a teacher and in charge of the class by "playing favorites." You were not fair. Accept all appropriate responses.)

Remember that part of being fair is not abusing any power or assignment you are given and not taking advantage of others.

▸ If time permits, you may begin the scenarios (pages 113-116) now or you may present the scenarios during a subsequent class period.

▸ Introduce the scenarios by saying:

Let's look at the role-plays and see if we can guide Alex and Maddie by using what we know about being fair and not taking advantage of others.

SCENARIO SUGGESTIONS:

1. Choose one or more scenarios. Read each chosen scenario to the students. Allow time for discussion after each scenario. Continue the discussion as long as the students offer choices and guidance for Maddie and Alex.

2. Divide the class into groups. Have each group role-play a different scenario illustrating choices based on good character traits. Allow time for discussion after each role-play.

3. Have the students read each scenario. After each scenario has been read, use the following questions to stimulate class discussion.

SUGGESTED SCENARIO DISCUSSION QUESTIONS:

Scenario #35

1. *What is the situation or dilemma that Alex is facing?* (The teacher wants to give credit to only Alex for an idea that Alex, Mike, and Chris thought up together.)

2. *What are Alex's choices?* (Alex can continue to let Mrs. Stidvent believe that the idea was his alone. Alex can clarify the situation for Mrs. Stidvent by telling her that the idea was his, Mike, and Chris's.)

3. *Have you ever been tempted to take credit for an idea or for something that you did not do yourself? What did you choose to do? Was that a fair decision?* (Accept all appropriate responses. Keep the students on the topic of not taking advantage of others.)

4. *What other character traits are in question in this role-play?* (Besides fairness and not taking advantage of others, honesty and trustworthiness are also involved.)

5. *What should Alex choose to say or do?* (Alex should tell Mrs. Stidvent that Mike and Chris were also involved in developing the idea. Accept all other appropriate responses.)

Scenario #36

1. *What is the situation or dilemma that Alex is facing?* (Alex has finished his popsicle and has noticed that other students are getting in line for "seconds." Alex would like another one himself.)

2. *What are Alex's choices?* (Alex can get in line and get another popsicle. Alex can not take advantage of the PTA and can be satisfied with one popsicle.)

3. *What character traits are involved besides fairness and not taking advantage of others?* (The other character traits involved are trustworthiness and honesty. By getting in line a second time, Alex is saying he never got the first popsicle and is taking advantage of the PTA.)

4. *Have you ever been faced with a similar situation? How did you handle it? Do you feel that your decision was fair?* (Accept all appropriate responses. Keep the students on the topic of being fair by not taking advantage of others.)

5. *What should Alex choose to say or do?* (Alex should be happy with his popsicle and thank the members of the PTA for it. Accept all other appropriate responses.)

Scenario #37

1. *What is the dilemma or problem that Maddie is facing?* (Sharon is taking advantage of the group by not working. Maddie does not think that this is fair.)

2. *What are Maddie's choices?* (Maddie can say nothing and just keep working. Maddie can tell Sharon that she is not being fair to the group. Maddie can speak with the teacher. Maddie can talk with her parents and get some guidance from them on what to do.)

3. ***Have you ever been in a similar situation? How did you choose to handle the situation? Do you feel that you handled the situation with fairness?*** (Accept all appropriate responses. Keep the students on the topic of not taking advantage of others.)

4. ***What should Maddie choose to say or do?*** (Maddie should talk with the teacher. Maddie can also speak with her parents or another adult whom she trusts. Accept all other appropriate responses.)

Scenario #38

1. ***What is the dilemma or problem that Maddie is facing?*** (Maddie does not like Mike and Chris. She wants to give them fewer pencils than the rest of the class.)

2. ***What are Maddie's choices?*** (Maddie can take advantage of the teacher's trust and decide to punish Chris and Mike by not giving them the same number of pencils as the rest of the class. Maddie can be fair and *not* take advantage of the teacher's trust and give every student in the class the same number of pencils.)

3. ***Have you ever been in a similar situation? What did you choose to do? Was that a decision based on the trait of fairness and not taking advantage of others or of their trust?*** (Accept all appropriate responses. Keep the students on the topic of being fair and not taking advantage of others or of their trust.)

4. ***What should Maddie choose to say or do?*** (Maddie should be fair, not take advantage of the teacher's trust, and give all the students the same number of pencils. Accept all other appropriate responses.)

Follow-Up Activities:

▸ Ask the students to keep a journal for a week and document specific times in their interactions with others that they consciously worked at being fair and not taking advantage of others or of their trust.

▸ Give each student paper and a pencil. Have the students write original scenarios demonstrating being fair by not taking advantage of others or of their trust.

SCENARIO #35

Alex, Mike, and Chris have been talking about a new idea for a class service project. Alex stays a few minutes after school today to share the idea with Mrs. Stidvent, his teacher. Mrs. Stidvent thinks the idea for the class service project is terrific. She seems to think Alex came up with the idea by himself and offers Alex extra-credit points on his grade.

What should Alex choose to say or do?

SCENARIO #36

The PTA is giving free popsicles to all the students as they leave school today. Alex is one of the first students in line and finishes his popsicle right away. He notices that some other students who have finished their popsicles have gotten back in line for a second one.

What should Alex choose to say or do?

 ALEX & MADDIE: LIFE-SKILL LESSONS THROUGH ROLE-PLAY © 2006 MAR*CO PRODUCTS, INC. 1-800-448-2197

SCENARIO #37

Maddie, Sharon, Maria, Tiffanye, and Ronnye are working in a cooperative group on a project for social studies. Everyone in the group except Sharon is doing her share of the work. Sharon just sits around and plays. The teacher, Mrs. Garcia, has told the class that everyone will get the same grade as the others in his/her group.

What should Maddie choose to say or do?

SCENARIO #38

Mrs. Peyton, Maddie's teacher, asks Maddie to distribute the same number of pencils to everyone in the class. Mike and Chris are two of the boys in the class. Maddie thinks Mike and Chris are silly and sometimes they are mean to her. When Maddie gets to their desks, she thinks about giving them fewer pencils than she has given the other students.

What should Maddie choose to say or do?

 ALEX & MADDIE: LIFE-SKILL LESSONS THROUGH ROLE-PLAY © 2006 MAR•CO PRODUCTS, INC. 1-800-448-2197

LISTEN TO OTHERS AND KEEP AN OPEN MIND

Purpose:

The students will learn the importance of listening in order to be fair and will practice listening to each other. After reading or role-playing the scenarios, the students will apply this knowledge to guide Alex and Maddie to make decisions based on *listening with an open mind*.

Materials Needed:

For the leader:
   None

For each student:
- ☐ Copy of *Scenario #39* (optional, page 120)
- ☐ Copy of *Scenario #40* (optional, page 121)
- ☐ Paper (optional)
- ☐ Pencil (optional)

Pre-Presentation Preparation:

Optional: Make a copy of the chosen scenarios for each student or for each student group.

Procedure:

Note: This lesson may be presented during one or more class periods.

▸ Ask for a student volunteer to come to the front of the classroom, face the class, and tell the students a little about his/her hobbies. After the student has finished, ask:

   What did (<u>NAME OF STUDENT</u>) say? (Accept all appropriate responses.)

   Did you notice anything about his/her body language? (The way the student spoke—facial expressions, stance, volume of voice, inflection in voice.)

   The body language you noticed is also part of listening skills. (Spend a little time discussing the importance of listening completely to another person and keeping an open mind.)

▶ Continue with two or three more volunteers, asking the following questions: (You may use your own questions if you prefer.)

1. *What did you do last weekend?*
2. *What are your favorite foods?*
3. *What makes you angry?*
4. *What makes you smile?*

▶ Then ask:

As we practiced listening to one of our class members, did you find your listening skills improving? If you did, can you tell us how? (Accept all appropriate responses.)

Being fair includes listening to others with an open mind.

▶ If time permits, you may begin the scenarios (pages 120-121) now or you may present the scenarios during a subsequent class period.

▶ Introduce the scenarios by saying:

Let's look at the role-plays and see if we can guide Alex and Maddie by using what we know about being fair by listening to others and keeping an open mind.

SCENARIO SUGGESTIONS:

1. Choose one or more scenarios. Read each chosen scenario to the students. Allow time for discussion after each scenario. Continue the discussion as long as the students offer choices and guidance for Maddie and Alex.

2. Divide the class into groups. Have each group role-play a different scenario illustrating choices based on good character traits. Allow time for discussion after each role-play.

3. Have the students read each scenario. After each scenario has been read, use the following questions to stimulate class discussion.

SUGGESTED SCENARIO DISCUSSION QUESTIONS:

Scenario #39

1. *What is the dilemma or problem that Alex and Maddie are facing?* (Alex and Maddie do not agree on how to spend the money their grandparents gave them to buy a Mother's Day gift for their mother.)

2. *What are Maddie's choices?* (Maddie can be stubborn and insist that her idea is the best without listening to Alex's ideas. Maddie can really listen to Alex.)

3. ***What are Alex's choices?*** (Alex can be stubborn and insist that his idea is the best without listening to Maddie's ideas. Alex can really listen to Maddie.)

4. ***Have you ever had to work out a disagreement? How did you handle it? Do you feel that you handled it fairly?*** (Accept all appropriate responses. Keep the students on the topic of being fair by listening to others and keeping an open mind.)

5. ***What should Alex and Maddie choose to say or do?*** (Maddie and Alex need to listen to each other's ideas and compromise [work together] to come up with an idea on how to spend the money. Accept all other appropriate responses.)

Scenario #40

1. ***What is the dilemma or problem that Alex is facing?*** (Alex and Frank each think that his idea for the class project is the best.)

2. ***What are Alex's choices?*** (Alex can continue to insist that his idea is the best or he can listen with an open mind to Frank's idea.)

3. ***Have you ever been faced with a similar situation? How did you handle the situation? Do you feel that you handled it with fairness?*** (Accept all appropriate responses. Keep the students on the topic of being fair by listening to others' ideas with an open mind.)

4. ***What should Alex choose to say or do?*** (Alex should listen to Frank's idea with an open mind and then share his ideas with Frank. Alex should stress to Frank that they both have good ideas and that if they work together, they can compromise and come up with one great idea. Accept all other appropriate responses.)

Follow-Up Activities:

▸ Ask the students to keep a journal documenting specific times during this week that they consciously work at listening with an open mind to others. Have the students share their thoughts at the next session.

▸ Give each student paper and a pencil. Have the students write original scenarios on the topic of listening to others with an open mind.

▸ Revisit the class definition for *fair* and check to see if the students feel a need for revisions, additions, or changes.

SCENARIO #39

Alex and Maddie's grandmother and grandfather have sent them some money to help them buy a gift for their mother on Mother's Day. Alex wants to buy a cookbook. Maddie wants to get her a new CD that their mom has been wanting. They can't agree on what to get her. Each of them thinks that his/her idea is best. Grandma and Grandpa said that they had to agree on one gift.

What should Alex and Maddie choose to say or do?

 ALEX & MADDIE: LIFE-SKILL LESSONS THROUGH ROLE-PLAY © 2006 MAR*CO PRODUCTS, INC. 1-800-448-2197

SCENARIO #40

Alex and Frank have been paired to work on a class project together. They are both good students. Each of them has some very good ideas for the assignment. However, neither one of them will listen to the other's ideas, because each boy thinks that his ideas are the best.

What should Alex choose to say or do?

FAIRNESS

_____

was caught showing
good character when
displaying *fairness* by

_____

_____

_____

Date _____

Signature _____

CARING

Topic Objectives:

To help children realize the value of:

Helping others in need.

Showing kindness and compassion.

Readily forgiving others.

Showing gratitude to others.

INTRODUCTION

Purpose:

To help students understand the meaning of *caring*

Materials Needed:

For the leader:
- ☐ Chart paper and marker
- ☐ Masking tape
- ☐ Dictionary (optional)

For each student:
    None

Pre-Presentation Preparation:

    None

DEFINITION OF
Caring

Caring: interest in, concern for

Procedure:

▸ Introduce the topic by having the students define, in their own words, what *caring* means to them. Guide the students to a definition.

    Possible example: Caring means being nice to others.

▸ After the students have agreed on a class definition of *caring*, write the definition on chart paper and post the paper in a place in the classroom where everyone can see it for future reference. The students may want to revise or add to the definition as the lessons on caring progress. You may give them the definition found above or the dictionary definition. Compare their definition to the formal definition. Make any changes the students or you believe are necessary at this time.

CARING: LESSON 1
SHOWING KINDNESS AND COMPASSION

Purpose:

The students will evaluate their own kindness and compassion and discuss ways in which to improve them. After reading or role-playing the scenarios, the students will apply their understanding of kindness and compassion to guide Alex and Maddie through several situations.

Materials Needed:

For the leader:
☐ Copy of *Kindness And Compassion Quiz* (page 129)

For each student:
☐ Paper or copy of *Kindness And Compassion Quiz* (page 129)
☐ Pencil
☐ Copy of *Scenario #41* (optional, page 130)
☐ Copy of *Scenario #42* (optional, page 131)
☐ Copy of *Scenario #43* (optional, page 132)
☐ Copy of *Scenario #44* (optional, page 133)
☐ Paper (optional)

Pre-Presentation Preparation:

Make a copy of the *Kindness And Compassion Quiz* for the leader.

Optional: Make a copy of the *Kindness And Compassion Quiz* for each student.

Optional: Make a copy of the chosen scenarios for each student or for each student group.

Procedure:

Note: This lesson may be presented during one or more class periods.

▶ Distribute a pencil and a piece of paper or a copy of the *Kindness And Compassion Quiz* to each student. Then say:

> *Number your paper from 1 to 10. I will be reading a series of questions. Answer each one by writing* yes *or* no.

or

> *Complete this quiz. Answer each question by writing* yes *or* no.

▸ Read each item on the *Kindness And Compassion Quiz*. (Options: You may read the questions aloud and have the students tally their responses of *yes* or *no*, or you may make a copy of the *Kindness And Compassion Quiz* for each student.)

▸ When you are finished, say:

> ***Count the number of yes responses you have.*** (Pause for the students to complete the task.) ***That number is your kindness/compassion number.***
>
> ***Do you feel that you need to work harder in the area of kindness and compassion?*** (Accept all appropriate responses. Keep the students on the topic of being kind and compassionate.)
>
> ***How can people improve their actions for displaying kindness and compassion? Where do they begin?*** (Everyone begins with baby steps. They must really think about other people and how they feel. Accept all appropriate responses and keep the students on the topic of being kind and compassionate.)
>
> ***Remember your kindness/compassion number. We will take this quiz again later and see if your number has changed.***

▸ If time permits, you may begin the scenarios (pages 130-133) now or you may present the scenarios during a subsequent class period.

▸ Introduce the scenarios by saying:

> ***Let's look at the role-plays and see if we can guide Alex and Maddie by using what we know about ways to show kindness and compassion.***

SCENARIO SUGGESTIONS:

1. Choose one or more scenarios. Read each chosen scenario to the students. Allow time for discussion after each scenario. Continue the discussion as long as the students offer choices and guidance for Maddie and Alex.

2. Divide the class into groups. Have each group role-play a different scenario illustrating choices based on good character traits. Allow time for discussion after each role-play.

3. Have the students read each scenario. After each scenario has been read, use the following questions to stimulate class discussion.

SUGGESTED SCENARIO DISCUSSION QUESTIONS:

Scenario #41

1. ***What is the dilemma or problem that Maddie is facing?*** (Maddie has noticed that Melissa, the new student, has no friends to eat lunch with. Maddie's friends want to ignore the situation.)

2. ***What are Maddie's choices?*** (Maddie can ignore the situation, just like her friends are doing. Maddie can think about how she would feel if she were in a similar situation and can invite Melissa to eat with her group. Maddie can eat with Melissa.)

3. ***Has this ever happened to you? What did you do? Did you handle the situation with kindness and compassion?*** (Accept all appropriate responses. Keep the students on the topic of making choices based on kindness and compassion.)

4. ***What should Maddie choose to say or do?*** (Maddie should find a way to include Melissa in her group. Accept all other appropriate responses.)

Scenario #42

1. ***What is the situation or problem that Maddie is facing?*** (Victor is making fun of Ronnye.)

2. ***What are Maddie's choices?*** (Maddie can also make fun of Ronnye and encourage the other team members to do the same. Maddie can tell Victor to stop making fun of Ronnye and remind him that they are a team. Maddie can tell Victor that not everyone is like everyone else and that he shouldn't put people down.)

3. ***Can you remember a time that you witnessed a similar situation? What did you do? Do you feel that you based your choice on kindness and compassion?*** (Accept all appropriate responses. Keep the students on the topic of making choices based on kindness and compassion.)

4. ***What should Maddie choose to say or do?*** (Maddie should do whatever she can to let Victor know that his actions are inappropriate and that he is not showing kindness or compassion. Accept all other appropriate responses.)

Scenario #43

1. ***What is the dilemma or problem that Alex is facing?*** (Willie is making fun of Victor for bringing a burrito for lunch every day.)

2. ***What are Alex's choices?*** (Alex can ignore the whole situation. Alex can tell Willie to stop making fun of Victor's lunch.)

3. ***Have you ever seen this happen to someone else or even to yourself? What did you do? Was your choice based on kindness and compassion?*** (Accept all appropriate responses. Keep the students on the topic of making choices based on kindness and compassion.)

4. ***What should Alex choose to say or do?*** (Alex should tell Willie to stop making fun of Victor's lunch. Accept all other appropriate responses.)

Scenario #44

1. ***What is the dilemma or problem that Maddie is facing?*** (Rebecca looks sad because she is not receiving many valentines.)

2. ***What are Maddie's choices?*** (Maddie can just count her own valentines and be happy that she received so many. Maddie can ignore Rebecca. Maddie can talk with Rebecca and maybe make her feel better, by letting her know she has a friend. Maddie can let the teacher know that there is a problem.)

3. ***What have you done in a similar situation? Could you have done more? Was the way that you chose to handle the situation based on kindness and compassion?*** (Accept all appropriate responses. Keep the students on the topic of making choices based on kindness and compassion.)

4. ***What should Maddie choose to say or do?*** (Maddie should try to find a way to make Rebecca feel better. It might be necessary for Maddie to let the teacher know that there is a problem. Accept all other appropriate responses.)

Follow-Up Activities:

▸ Administer the *Kindness And Compassion Quiz* again and see if the students' kindness/compassion numbers have changed. Discuss any changes.

▸ Ask the students to do three kind and compassionate actions and notice the reactions of others. Have them record their actions and others' responses and share at the next lesson what they experienced.

▸ Give each student paper and a pencil. Have the students write original scenarios on the topics of kindness and compassion.

▸ Students may work individually or in groups to write new *Kindness And Compassion Quizzes.*

KINDNESS AND COMPASSION QUIZ

1. Have you ever helped a hurt animal? _____

2. Have you ever helped someone who had fallen? _____

3. When your mom or dad looks tired, have you ever offered to do more for him or her? _____

4. Have you ever done a chore at home or at school when it wasn't even your chore or your turn to do it? _____

5. Have you ever played with a young child when you really would rather have done something else? _____

6. Have you ever offered to do extra work just to help someone else out? _____

7. Have you ever helped a young student at school whom you didn't even know? _____

8. Have you ever given your toys or money to charity? _____

9. Have you ever opened the door for another person, and let him or her go through the door ahead of you? _____

10. Have you ever helped a fellow student understand an assignment? _____

TOTAL *YES* RESPONSES:

SCENARIO #41

Melissa is a new student in Maddie's classroom. She came from another state. Maddie notices that at lunch Melissa is sitting and eating all by herself. Maddie mentions this to the girls that she is having lunch with. They tell Maddie not to worry about it. They say that Melissa will make friends eventually and they continue eating and talking.

What should Maddie choose to say or do?

     ALEX & MADDIE: LIFE-SKILL LESSONS THROUGH ROLE-PLAY © 2006 MAR*CO PRODUCTS, INC. 1-800-448-2197

SCENARIO #42

During physical education class, Mrs. Hillmon, the coach, has the students pick teams for a soccer game. Coach chooses Mike and Tiffanye as team captains. Mike selects Maddie and Victor to be on his team. Tiffanye chooses Chris and Melissa. After Mike and Tiffanye choose sides, Ronnye is the only student who hasn't been picked. Mike picks Ronnye for his team. Victor starts making faces, because Ronnye can't run very fast.

What should Maddie choose to say or do?

SCENARIO #43

The boys in 5C always sit together for lunch in the cafeteria. Most of the boys buy their lunch at school. Victor always brings his lunch from home. It is always a homemade burrito and a can of juice. Lately, Willie has started making fun of Victor's lunch and asking Victor if his family is poor. A couple of the other boys have also begun making fun of Victor. Victor seems embarrassed.

What should Alex choose to say or do?

ALEX & MADDIE: LIFE-SKILL LESSONS THROUGH ROLE-PLAY © 2006 MAR*CO PRODUCTS, INC. 1-800-448-2197

SCENARIO #44

During the Valentine exchange in Maddie's class, Maddie notices that Rebecca, the new girl, is not receiving many Valentines. Rebecca looks like she wants to cry.

What should Maddie choose to say or do?

CARING: LESSON 2
HELP OTHERS IN NEED

Purpose:

The students will learn that genuine helping is not driven by wanting something in return. After reading or role-playing the scenarios, the students will discuss this idea and apply this knowledge to help Alex and Maddie to make caring choices by genuinely helping others.

Materials Needed:

For the leader:
   None

For each student:
   ☐ Pencil and paper for upper grades
   ☐ Crayons and drawing paper for lower grades
   ☐ Copy of *Scenario #45* (optional, page 138)
   ☐ Copy of *Scenario #46* (optional, page 139)
   ☐ Copy of *Scenario #47* (optional, page 140)
   ☐ Copy of *Scenario #48* (optional, page 141)
   ☐ Copy of *Scenario #49* (optional, page 142)
   ☐ Copy of *Caring Commitment Card* (optional, page 143)

Pre-Presentation Preparation:

Make a copy of the *Caring Commitment Card* for each student.

Optional: Make a copy of the chosen scenarios for each student or for each student group.

Procedure:

Note: This lesson may be presented during one or more class periods.

▸ Distribute paper and a pencil or drawing paper and crayons to each student. Introduce the lesson by saying:

> *It is important to help other people for no other reason than just because. You should not want special attention or special rewards because you have helped someone. Some people do nice or caring things to get attention. Really caring people do things for others just because it is the right thing to do. They don't*

care if they will be noticed or even rewarded. Sometimes they do things quietly or secretly and no one notices who did the good deed.

For the next 5-10 minutes, write down ways (the lower-grade students can draw pictures instead) *that you could help others without looking for recognition. Then you will share your ideas with the class.*

▸ When the allotted time has elapsed, have the students share their ideas.

▸ If the whole class feels passionately about an idea that is presented, perhaps this could be a project you could spearhead. (Examples—picking up litter at lunch, collecting toys for a local shelter, collecting canned goods for the Rescue Mission, etc.)

▸ If time permits, you may begin the scenarios (pages 138-142) now or you may present the scenarios during a subsequent class period.

▸ Introduce the scenarios by saying:

Let's look at the role-plays and see if we can guide Alex and Maddie by using what we know about helping others just because it is the right thing to do.

SCENARIO SUGGESTIONS:

1. Choose one or more scenarios. Read each chosen scenario to the students. Allow time for discussion after each scenario. Continue the discussion as long as the students offer choices and guidance for Maddie and Alex.

2. Divide the class into groups. Have each group role-play a different scenario illustrating choices based on good character traits. Allow time for discussion after each role-play.

3. Have the students read each scenario. After each scenario has been read, use the following questions to stimulate class discussion.

SUGGESTED SCENARIO DISCUSSION QUESTIONS:

Scenario #45

1. *What is the situation or problem that Maddie is facing?* (Maddie has to decide if she cares enough to stop playing and help someone who is hurt.)

2. *What are Maddie's choices?* (Maddie can be like the others and ignore the small child. Maddie can stop and help the small child who is hurt.)

3. *Have you ever been in a similar situation? What did you do? How did you feel about the way you handled the problem?* (Accept all appropriate responses. Keep the students on the topic of being caring by genuinely helping others.)

4. **What should Maddie choose to say or do?** (Maddie should stop playing and help the small child who is hurt. Accept all other appropriate responses.)

Scenario #46

1. **What is the dilemma or problem that Alex is facing?** (Alex is facing some peer pressure not to help in the class cleanup.)

2. **What are Alex's choices?** (Alex can listen to Bill and not clean up. Alex can follow the teacher's directions and help clean up the classroom.)

3. **What other character traits are involved in this situation?** (By cleaning up the classroom, the students are also demonstrating *responsibility*. By following the directions of the teacher, the students are also showing *respect*. Accept all appropriate responses.)

4. **Has a similar situation ever happened to you? How did you handle the situation? Do you feel that you handled it well?** (Accept all appropriate responses. Keep the students on the topic of being caring by genuinely helping others.)

5. **What should Alex choose to say or do?** (Alex should help by cleaning up the classroom. Accept all other appropriate responses.)

Scenario #47

1. **What is the situation or problem that Maddie is facing?** (Maddie would like to keep the game for herself.)

2. **What are Maddie's choices?** (Maddie can talk her mother into letting her keep the game. Maddie can just keep the game and not tell her mother. Maddie can donate the game as she is supposed to.)

3. **Have you ever wanted something that was bought for someone or something else? What did you do? Was your choice filled with the trait of caring?** (Accept all appropriate responses. Keep the students on the topic of being caring by genuinely helping others.)

4. **What should Maddie choose to say or do?** (Maddie should donate the game. Accept all other appropriate responses.)

Scenario #48

1. **What is the dilemma or situation that Alex is facing?** (Alex noticed that his teacher, Ms. Baitland, looks unhappy.)

2. **What are Alex's choices?** (Alex can forget that he notices Ms. Baitland looks like something is bothering her. Alex can say or do something nice for Ms. Baitland.)

3. **Have you ever been in a similar situation? What did you do? How do you feel about your choice? Could you have been more caring?** (Accept all appropriate responses. Keep students on the topic of helping others in need.)

4. **What should Alex choose to say or do?** (Alex should let Ms. Baitland know that he hopes she feels better. Accept all other appropriate responses.)

Scenario #49

1. **What is the problem or dilemma that Maddie is facing?** (Maddie notices that her mom is looking really tired tonight.)

2. **What are Maddie's choices?** (Maddie can ask her mom what is wrong. Maddie can ask her mom if she can give her some extra help tonight. Maddie can do nothing and just forget that she noticed that her mom looks tired.)

3. **What have you done in a similar situation? How did you feel about the way you handled the situation? Could you have done more?** (Accept all appropriate responses. Keep the students on the topic of being caring by genuinely helping others.)

4. **What should Maddie choose to say or do?** (Maddie should ask her mom if she is okay. Maddie should offer to give her mom some extra help tonight. Accept all other appropriate responses.)

Follow-Up Activities:

▸ Distribute a *Caring Commitment Card* to each student. Then say:

> **Decide on a caring act that you are willing to perform. Write that act on the card, then sign your name and today's date. Give the card to someone in the room. No person may receive more than one card.**

At a later date, have the students describe how these caring acts made them feel and how they think their caring acts made the recipients feel.

▸ Give each student paper and a pencil. Have the students write original scenarios on the topic of being caring by genuinely helping others.

SCENARIO #45

Maddie is playing outside during lunch recess and notices that a small child has fallen and cut her leg. Everyone in Maddie's group is having a great time playing hopscotch. Others in Maddie's group also notice the little one with the bloody knee, but continue to play and ignore her.

What should Maddie choose to say or do?

 ALEX & MADDIE: LIFE-SKILL LESSONS THROUGH ROLE-PLAY © 2006 MAR*CO PRODUCTS, INC. 1-800-448-2197

SCENARIO #46

It is almost time for the class to be dismissed for the day. Mrs. Peyton has asked the class to help pick up trash and tidy up the room before the bell rings. Bill says he thinks this is the custodian's job and why should he be asked to do it? Bill is quietly telling all the boys around him, including Alex, not to help.

What should Alex choose to say or do?

SCENARIO #47

Maddie's school is having a toy drive for the local Child Crisis Center. Maddie's mother bought a game for Maddie to donate. Maddie really likes the game and would like to keep it for herself.

What should Maddie choose to say or do?

 ALEX & MADDIE: LIFE-SKILL LESSONS THROUGH ROLE-PLAY © 2006 MAR*CO PRODUCTS, INC. 1-800-448-2197

SCENARIO #48

Alex noticed that when Ms. Baitland walked into the classroom today she was not smiling like she normally does. He decides that she is feeling sick or maybe unhappy about something.

What should Alex choose to say or do?

SCENARIO #49

When Mom gets home, Maddie notices that she looks really tired.

What should Maddie choose to say or do?

 ALEX & MADDIE: LIFE-SKILL LESSONS THROUGH ROLE-PLAY © 2006 MAR*CO PRODUCTS, INC. 1-800-448-2197

CARING COMMITMENT CARD

I will _____

_____

_____ .

Name _____

Date _____

CARING COMMITMENT CARD

I will _____

_____

_____ .

Name _____

Date _____

CARING: LESSON 3
FORGIVING OTHERS

Purpose:

The students will learn that readily forgiving others is another way to show caring. After reading or role-playing the scenarios, the students will apply their knowledge of forgiveness to help guide Alex and Maddie through several situations.

Materials Needed:

For the leader:
- ☐ Chalkboard, chalk, and eraser or chart paper and marker
- ☐ Potatoes or rocks
- ☐ Plastic grocery bag

For each student:
- ☐ Copy of *Scenario #50* (optional, page 147)
- ☐ Copy of *Scenario #51* (optional, page 148)
- ☐ Paper (optional)
- ☐ Pencil (optional)

Pre-Presentation Preparation:

Optional: Make a copy of the chosen scenarios for each student or for each student group.

Procedure:

Note: This lesson may be presented during one or more class periods.

▸ Introduce the lesson by saying:

> *Today we will be talking about forgiving others for hurtful things that they say or do. Without saying anyone's name, please share with us some of the things others have said or done that hurt your feelings.*

▸ Ask a student volunteer to hold the plastic bag so it is easily visible. Write the students' contributions on the chalkboard/chart paper. As you write, put a potato or rock into the plastic bag for each student contribution. Then say:

> *It looks like our bag is getting very heavy. As you can see and (<u>NAME OF THE STUDENT VOLUNTEER</u>) can feel, if you keep all the hurtful things inside you, you*

will be carrying a heavy burden. Let's see what happens as we forgive others. For those of you who shared, let's revisit the things others have said or done that hurt your feelings. As we do, tell us if you were able to quickly forgive the person.

▸ For every student who says he/she was able to forgive, take one potato or rock out of the bag and erase the hurt from the chalkboard or cross the hurt off the chart paper.

▸ Redirect the students' attention to the bag and ask:

What do you notice about the bag now that we have forgiven others? (It is lighter. It is easier to go about our day without all the hurts. Accept all appropriate responses and keep the students on the topic of forgiving others.)

What is the message in this lesson? (That we will feel better if we learn to forgive others. That remembering all those hurts weighs us down. Accept all appropriate responses. Keep the students on the topic of forgiving others.)

▸ If time permits, you may begin the scenarios (pages 147-148) now or you may present the scenarios during a subsequent class period.

▸ Introduce the scenarios by saying:

Let's look at the role-plays and see if we can guide Alex and Maddie by using what we know about forgiving others.

SCENARIO SUGGESTIONS:

1. Choose one or more scenarios. Read each chosen scenario to the students. Allow time for discussion after each scenario. Continue the discussion as long as the students offer choices and guidance for Maddie and Alex.

2. Divide the class into groups. Have each group role-play a different scenario illustrating choices based on good character traits. Allow time for discussion after each role-play.

3. Have the students read each scenario. After each scenario has been read, use the following questions to stimulate class discussion.

SUGGESTED SCENARIO DISCUSSION QUESTIONS:

Scenario #50

1. *What is the dilemma or problem that Alex is facing?* (Alex is still hurting over George's remark during the soccer game when Alex did not score.)

2. ***What are Alex's choices?*** (Alex can forgive and forget what George said. It was during the game and the game is over. Alex can talk with George about his remark. Alex can stop talking to George and stop being his friend.)

3. ***Has a similar situation ever happened to you? How did you handle the situation? Did you show the character trait of caring by forgiving the person who hurt you?*** (Accept all appropriate responses. Keep the students on the topic of displaying caring by forgiving others.)

4. ***What should Alex choose to say or do?*** (If Alex is still hurting, he can let George know that his comment really bothered him. Alex can just forget the comment and continue to be friends with George. If George is always calling others names when they make a mistake, Alex should let George know that this is offensive. Accept all other appropriate responses.)

Scenario #51

1. ***What is the dilemma or problem that Maddie is facing?*** (Brenda is trying to break up Maddie's friendships.)

2. ***What are Maddie's choices?*** (Maddie can get very angry with Brenda and refuse to talk with her any more or to be her friend. Maddie can talk with Brenda and ask her what is going on. Maddie can readily forgive Brenda for making a mistake.)

3. ***Have you ever been in a similar situation? How did you choose to handle the problem? Was your choice based on caring and readily forgiving others?*** (Accept all appropriate responses. Keep the students on the topic of displaying caring by readily forgiving others.)

4. ***What should Maddie choose to say or do?*** (Maddie should talk with Brenda, work out the misunderstanding, and forgive Brenda. Accept all other appropriate responses.)

Follow-Up Activities:

▸ Revisit the class definition for *caring* and check to see if the students feel a need for revisions, additions, or changes.

▸ Keep the plastic bag in a prominent place in the classroom to remind the students to let go of *hurts* and readily forgive others.

▸ Give each student paper and a pencil. Have the students write original scenarios showing choices that involve forgiving others.

SCENARIO #50

Alex is playing soccer at recess. He misses a clear shot and does not score a goal. George calls Alex a "choker," someone who cannot finish a score. Alex is hurt and embarrassed. The boys continue playing until the bell to return to class rings. Alex is still hurt by George's remark. George is acting like nothing was said.

What should Alex choose to say or do?

SCENARIO #51

Brenda, a student in Maddie's class, has told Tiffanye and Jessica not to be Maddie's friends any more. Tiffanye and Jessica told Maddie what Brenda said. Maddie is very hurt and angry.

What should Maddie choose to say or do?

CARING

_____

was caught showing
good character when
displaying *caring* by

_____

_____

_____

Date _____

Signature _____

CITIZENSHIP

Topic Objectives:

To help children realize the value of:

Showing respect for the United States flag.

Doing their part to make their family, school,
and community a better place and to take care of the environment.

Informing themselves and voting in school elections.

Helping their neighbors.

Being ready to cooperate.

Obeying rules and laws.

CITIZENSHIP
INTRODUCTION

Purpose:

To help students understand the meaning of *citizenship*

Materials Needed:

For the leader:
- ☐ Chart paper and marker
- ☐ Masking tape
- ☐ Dictionary (optional)

For each student:
  None

Pre-Presentation Preparation:

  None

DEFINITION OF
Citizenship, Citizen

Citizenship: behaving in a respectful manner toward a country's laws and environment

Citizen: An inhabitant of a city or country, a person regarded as a member of a sovereign state, entitled to its protection and subject to its laws

Procedure:

▸ Introduce the topic by having the students define, in their own words, what *citizenship* means to them. Guide the students to a definition.

> Possible example: A person showing good citizenship would take care of his/her community, vote, help others, obey rules, and show respect for authority.

▸ After the students have agreed on a class definition of *citizenship*, write the definition on chart paper and post the paper in a place in the classroom where everyone can see it for future reference. The students may want to revise or add to the definition as the lessons on citizenship progress. You may give them the definition found above or the dictionary definition. Compare their definition to the formal definition. Make any changes the students or you believe are necessary at this time.

RESPECT FOR OUR UNITED STATES FLAG

Purpose:

The students will learn the rules and regulations concerning the flag of the United States. After reading or role-playing the scenarios, the students will apply this knowledge to help Alex and Maddie. (*Note:* Other countries will also have similar rules and procedures for their flags.)

Materials Needed:

For the leader:
- ☐ Copy of *Rules And Procedures For The United States Flag* (page 156)

For each student:
- ☐ Copy of *Scenario #52* (optional, page 157)
- ☐ Copy of *Scenario #53* (optional, page 158)
- ☐ Copy of *Scenario #54* (optional, page 159)
- ☐ Paper (optional)
- ☐ Pencil (optional)

Pre-Presentation Preparation:

Make a copy of the *Rules And Procedures For The United States Flag* for the leader.

Optional: Make a copy of the chosen scenarios for each student or for each student group.

Procedure:

Note: This lesson may be presented during one or more class periods.

▸ Depending on the grade level, select two to four rules concerning the rules and regulations for the flag of the United States that are most important/relevant to teach to your students. As you read each of the selected rules, have the students describe, in their own words, its application. In rule #2, for example, the students might say that the flag should not be allowed to get soiled or dirty by touching the ground.

▸ Have the students cite examples in which they have seen a rule followed or disregarded.

▸ Remind the students that all countries have flags and that we must show reverence and respect for the flags of other countries.

▸ If time permits, you may begin the scenarios (pages 157-159) now or you may present the scenarios during a subsequent class period.

▸ Introduce the scenarios by saying:

Let's look at the role-plays and see if we can guide Alex and Maddie by using what we know about showing respect for our nation's flag.

SCENARIO SUGGESTIONS:

1. Choose one or more scenarios. Read each chosen scenario to the students. Allow time for discussion after each scenario. Continue the discussion as long as the students offer choices and guidance for Maddie and Alex.

2. Divide the class into groups. Have each group role-play a different scenario illustrating choices based on good character traits. Allow time for discussion after each role-play.

3. Have the students read each scenario. After each scenario has been read, use the following questions to stimulate class discussion.

SUGGESTED SCENARIO DISCUSSION QUESTIONS:

Scenario #52

1. *What is the dilemma or problem that Alex is facing?* (Alex has noticed a hole in the United States flag hanging in the classroom.)

2. *What are Alex's choices?* (Alex can choose to simply ignore the hole in the flag and say nothing. Alex can let the teacher know about the hole.)

3. *Have you ever been in a similar situation? How did you handle the situation and did you show respect for the United States flag?* (Accept all appropriate responses. Keep the students on the topic of practicing good citizenship by showing respect for the United States flag.)

4. *What should Alex choose to say or do?* (Alex should let the teacher know, as soon as he is able, that the United States flag in the classroom has a hole in it. Accept all other appropriate responses.)

Scenario #53

1. *What is the dilemma or problem that Maddie is facing?* (Maddie has noticed that the United States flag is being flown upside down.)

2. ***What are Maddie's choices?*** (Maddie can simply ignore the fact that the flag is being flown incorrectly and go about her business. Maddie can let an adult at school know that the flag is being flown incorrectly.)

3. ***Have you ever been in a similar situation? Did you handle the situation by practicing good citizenship and alerting someone to the fact that our flag was being displayed incorrectly?*** (Accept all appropriate responses. Keep the students on the topic of displaying good citizenship by showing respect for the United States flag.)

4. ***What should Maddie choose to say or do?*** (Maddie should alert the school's main office that the United States flag is being flown incorrectly. Accept all other appropriate responses.)

Scenario #54

1. ***What is the problem or dilemma that Alex is facing?*** (The flag is being carried onto the field. Alex removes his cap and places it over his heart. His friend, Mario, does not.)

2. ***What are Alex's choices?*** (Alex can simply ignore the fact that Mario did not show respect for the United States flag by removing his cap and putting it over his heart. Alex can remind Mario to take off his cap and put it over his heart.)

3. ***Have you ever been in a similar situation? Did you handle the situation by practicing good citizenship and alerting someone to the fact that our flag was not being properly respected?*** (Accept all appropriate responses. Keep the students on the topic of displaying good citizenship by showing respect for the United States flag.)

4. ***What should Alex choose to say or do?*** (Alex should remind Mario to remove his cap and place it over his heart. Accept all other appropriate responses.)

Follow-Up Activities:

▸ Give each student paper and a pencil. Have the students write original scenarios focusing on showing respect for our nation's flag.

▸ Discuss how students could show respect for the flags of other countries even if they are not sure of the specific flag etiquette of those countries.

RULES AND PROCEDURES FOR THE UNITED STATES FLAG

1. The flag should never be displayed with the union down, except as a signal of dire distress in instances of extreme danger to life or property.

2. The flag should never touch anything beneath it, such as the ground, the floor, water, or merchandise.

3. The flag should never be carried flat or horizontally, but always aloft and free.

4. The flag should never be used as wearing apparel, bedding, or drapery. It should never be festooned, drawn back, nor up, in folds, but always allowed to fall free. Bunting of blue, white, and red, always arranged with the blue above, the white in the middle, and the red below, should be used for covering a speaker's desk, draping the front of the platform, and for decoration in general.

5. The flag should never be fastened, displayed, used, or stored in such a manner as to permit it to be easily torn, soiled, or damaged in any way.

6. The flag should never be used as a covering for a ceiling.

7. The flag should never have placed upon it, nor on any part of it, nor attached to it any mark, insignia, letter, word, figure, design, picture, or drawing of any nature.

8. The flag should never be used as a receptacle for receiving, holding, carrying, or delivering anything.

9. The flag should never be used for advertising purposes in any manner whatsoever. It should not be embroidered on such articles as cushions or handkerchiefs and the like, printed or otherwise impressed on paper napkins or boxes or anything that is designed for temporary use and discard. Advertising signs should not be fastened to a staff or halyard from which the flag is flown.

10. No part of the flag should ever be used as a costume or athletic uniform. However, a flag patch may be affixed to the uniform of military personnel, firefighters, police officers, and members of patriotic organizations. The flag represents a living country and is itself considered a living thing. Therefore, the lapel flag pin, being a replica, should be worn on the left lapel near the heart.

11. The flag, when it is in such condition that it is no longer a fitting emblem for display, should be destroyed in a dignified way, preferably by burning.

CONDUCT DURING HOISTING, LOWERING, OR PASSING THE FLAG

During the ceremony of hoisting or lowering the flag or when the flag is passing in a parade or in review, all persons present except those in uniform should face the flag and stand at attention with the right hand over the heart. Those present in uniform should render the military salute. When not in uniform, men should remove their headdress with their right hand and hold it to the left shoulder, the hand being over the heart. Aliens should stand at attention. The salute to the flag in a moving column should be rendered at the moment the flag passes.

SCENARIO #52

Alex notices that the United States flag in his classroom has a hole in its center. The hole is hard to see because of the way the flag hangs. Alex knows that the teacher is not aware of the hole.

What should Alex choose to say or do?

SCENARIO #53

Maddie has arrived at school and notices that the United States flag is upside down. The stars are facing down.

What should Maddie choose to say or do?

 ALEX & MADDIE: LIFE-SKILL LESSONS THROUGH ROLE-PLAY © 2006 MAR✷CO PRODUCTS, INC. 1-800-448-2197

SCENARIO #54

Alex and his friend, Mario, are at a ballgame. The United States flag is being carried in by the color guard. Everybody is standing up. Alex takes his cap off with his right hand and puts it over his heart. Mario does not.

What should Alex choose to say or do?

CITIZENSHIP: LESSON 2
DOING YOUR PART

Purpose:

Participating in the activity will show the students how each action or inaction affects others. After reading or role-playing the scenarios, the students will apply this knowledge and guide Alex and Maddie in making decisions based on the trait of good citizenship and helping all areas of their community.

Materials Needed:

For the leader:
- ☐ Multi-colored ball of thick yarn

For each student:
- ☐ Copy of *Scenario #55* (optional, page 164)
- ☐ Copy of *Scenario #56* (optional, page 165)
- ☐ Copy of *Scenario #57* (optional, page 166)
- ☐ Copy of *Scenario #58* (optional, page 167)
- ☐ Paper (optional)
- ☐ Pencil (optional)

Pre-Presentation Preparation:

Optional: Make a copy of the chosen scenarios for each student or for each student group.

Procedure:

Note: This lesson may be presented during one or more class periods.

▸ Make sure you have enough space for the students to sit in a large circle. Older students may stand. Have the students stand or sit in a circle. Ask for a volunteer. Then say to the volunteer and the class:

> *Take hold of one end of this yarn and wrap it around your index finger. The reason the yarn is multi-colored is to represent all the different ways we help in our communities.* Community *can mean home, school, city, nation, and/or world.*
>
> *Once you have wrapped the yarn around your index finger, roll the ball of yarn* (or toss it, if standing) *to someone on the other side of the circle. That person will*

take hold of the yarn, hold tight, and roll/toss the ball of yarn to someone else. When we are finished, everyone should be holding onto part of the yarn. Hold it firmly. (Pause for the students to complete the activity.)

We have now created an intertwined community with many different jobs and roles for us to play. Let's demonstrate how important each one of us is to the others in our communities. I will tug on a part of the intertwined community that we formed.

Who felt the tug? (Accept all appropriate responses.)

What would have happened if any one of you had let go of your yarn? (The yarn would have slipped and our intertwined community would have collapsed. Accept all appropriate responses.)

▸ Tug on the yarn several more times. Then say:

What must happen for communities to run in an orderly fashion? (Everyone must do his/her part.)

Can you think of ways you are intertwined with others in your community and how your actions affect those around you? (Accept all appropriate responses.)

Each one of us has or will have many different jobs and ways that we can help in our community. You have seen how important it is for us to hold that piece of yarn, do our part, and practice citizenship in all of our different communities— home, school, city, nation, and world. Remember to do your part, or you will let your community down.

▸ If time permits, you may begin the scenarios (pages 164-167) now or you may present the scenarios during a subsequent class period.

▸ Introduce the scenarios by saying:

Let's look at the role-plays and see if we can guide Alex and Maddie by using what we know about behaving in a manner that shows good citizenship.

SCENARIO SUGGESTIONS:

1. Choose one or more scenarios. Read each chosen scenario to the students. Allow time for discussion after each scenario. Continue the discussion as long as the students offer choices and guidance for Maddie and Alex.

2. Divide the class into groups. Have each group role-play a different scenario illustrating choices based on good character traits. Allow time for discussion after each role-play.

3. Have the students read each scenario. After each scenario has been read, use the following questions to stimulate class discussion.

SUGGESTED SCENARIO DISCUSSION QUESTIONS:

Scenario #55

1. *What is the situation or dilemma that Maddie is facing?* (Maddie knows that littering is not good, but she likes Brenda and does not want to offend her.)

2. *What are Maddie's choices?* (Maddie can simply ignore the fact that Brenda threw litter on the ground. Maddie can speak up and say that littering is bad. Maddie can pick up the litter and throw it away herself.)

3. *Can you remember a time that you were faced with a similar situation? What did you do? Did you display good citizenship?* (Accept all appropriate responses. Keep the students on the topic of displaying good citizenship by taking care of our environment—at school, in the community, in the classroom, etc.)

4. *What should Maddie choose to say or do?* (Maddie needs to point out to Brenda that she dropped something. Either Brenda picks it up or Maddie can pick it up and say she knows that Brenda accidentally dropped it. Accept all other appropriate responses.)

Scenario #56

1. *What is the situation or problem that Alex is facing?* (Jon and Larry want Alex to help them scribble on the posters and essays in the hall.)

2. *What are Alex's choices?* (Alex can help them vandalize and write on the posters in the hall. Alex can say *no* and walk away. Alex can talk with an adult whom he trusts and let that adult know what Jon and Larry are planning to do.)

3. *Can you remember a time when you were faced with a similar decision? What did you choose to do? Was your decision based on displaying good citizenship?* (Accept all appropriate responses. Keep the students on the topic of displaying good citizenship by taking care of our environment.)

4. *What should Alex choose to say or do?* (Alex should say *no* and walk away. He should let Jon and Larry know that this is wrong and that he will not be a part of it. He should also share this information with an adult whom he trusts. Accept all other appropriate responses.)

Scenario #57

1. *What is the dilemma or problem that Maddie and Alex are facing?* (Maddie and Alex have discovered three boys vandalizing their neighbor's garage door. They know who the boys are.)

2. *What are Maddie and Alex's choices?* (Maddie and Alex can ignore what they have just seen. Maddie and Alex can go home quickly and tell their parents what they have witnessed. Maddie and Alex can call the neighbors and let them know what is happening. Maddie and Alex can call the police.)

3. *Have you ever been in a similar situation? What did you do? Did you use the trait of good citizenship in your decision on handling the situation?* (Accept all appropriate responses. Keep the students on the topic of displaying good citizenship by taking care of their environment.)

4. *What should Maddie and Alex choose to say or do?* (Maddie and Alex should get to an adult whom they trust as quickly as possible. If they are unable to find one, they need to call the police. Accept all other appropriate responses.)

Scenario #58

1. *What is the situation or dilemma that Maddie is facing?* (Maddie hasn't heard her mom or dad mention voting and she knows that voting is an important part of being a good citizen.)

2. *What are Maddie's choices?* (Maddie can just not say anything. Maddie can respectfully ask her parents if they will be voting.)

3. *Have you ever been in a similar situation? How did you handle it? Do you feel that you handled the situation based on good citizenship?* (Accept all appropriate responses. Keep the students on the topic of being good citizens by voting in community and national elections.)

4. *What should Maddie choose to say or do?* (Maddie should respectfully ask/remind her parents to vote. Accept all other appropriate responses.)

Follow-Up Activity:

▸ Give each student paper and a pencil. Have the students write original scenarios focusing on the character trait of citizenship.

SCENARIO #55

Maddie and her friends just finished eating lunch together and are on their way to the playground for lunch recess. Brenda is finishing a candy bar and throws the wrapper on the playground. Maddie knows that littering is not the right thing to do, but she really likes Brenda as a friend and doesn't want to be called a "Goodie Goodie" by the group.

What should Maddie choose to say or do?

ALEX & MADDIE: LIFE-SKILL LESSONS THROUGH ROLE-PLAY © 2006 MAR*CO PRODUCTS, INC. 1-800-448-2197

SCENARIO #56

The winning posters and essays for the Character Contest have been posted in the hall next to the main office. Jon and Larry are angry because their posters were not selected. While in the boys restroom, they are discussing with Alex how they will scribble on the posters and essays with black markers each time they pass them. They want Alex to help them. Alex's poster and essay were not chosen, either.

What should Alex choose to say or do?

SCENARIO #57

While Alex and Maddie are walking their dog, Annie, they notice three older boys spray painting words on a neighbor's garage door. When the boys see Alex and Maddie, they run away. Alex and Maddie recognize the boys.

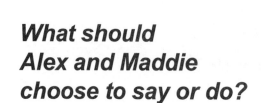

What should Alex and Maddie choose to say or do?

ALEX & MADDIE: LIFE-SKILL LESSONS THROUGH ROLE-PLAY © 2006 MAR∗CO PRODUCTS, INC. 1-800-448-2197

SCENARIO #58

The election for mayor in Maddie's city is being held this week. Maddie notices that her mom and dad have not mentioned anything about going to vote.

What should Maddie choose to say or do?

CITIZENSHIP: LESSON 3
HELPING YOUR NEIGHBORS

Purpose:

The students will list or draw various ways they can practice good citizenship by helping their neighbors/others at school or in the community. After reading or role-playing the scenarios, the students will apply their understanding of practicing good citizenship by helping others to guide Alex and Maddie.

Materials Needed:

For the leader:
- ☐ Chalkboard and chalk
- ☐ Timer

For each student:
- ☐ Pencil and paper for upper grades
- ☐ Crayons and drawing paper for lower grades
- ☐ Copy of *Scenario #59* (optional, page 172)
- ☐ Copy of *Scenario #60* (optional, page 173)
- ☐ Copy of *Scenario #61* (optional, page 174)
- ☐ Copy of *Scenario #62* (optional, page 175)

Pre-Presentation Preparation:

Optional: Make a copy of the chosen scenarios for each student or for each student group.

Procedure:

Note: This lesson may be presented during one or more class periods.

▸ Distribute paper and pencils or crayons to each student. Then give the following directions, pausing after each step for the students to complete the task:

Fold your sheet of paper in half lengthwise. Title the upper left-hand column "School" and the upper right-hand column "Community." List (draw) ways you can help in your school and in your community. (Give the students approximately 10 minutes to complete this part of the lesson.)

Please share with us some of the ways you have listed (drawn) that you feel you can help in either your school or your community. (Accept all appropriate responses.)

▸ Write the students' responses on the chalkboard under the column labeled "School" or "Community." Make note of any recurring ideas that are in your classroom. Then ask:

Do you notice any suggestions that are being made repeatedly by more than one of your classmates? (Accept all appropriate responses.)

Remember that as citizens of our community—be it home, school, neighborhood, nation, or world—we need to contribute. We need to help and do our share. Think about the list you created. Please circle one idea/picture on that list that you can commit to doing for one week. At our next meeting, we will revisit this lesson and you may share the commitment that you have circled and have kept for one week.

▸ *Optional:* Based on the list generated by your class, this may be the perfect moment to adopt one of the ideas listed as a classroom project. (Examples: cleaning an area around the school, adopting a lower-grade classroom to read stories to, collecting items for a local charity or food bank, etc. If this is of interest, ask:

Is there any one of these ideas that you feel strongly about as a class?

Is there an idea that our class could adopt to help in our school or in our community? (If one of the ideas presented elicits class interest and energy, determine whether it would be a good class project.)

▸ If time permits, you may begin the scenarios (pages 172-175) now or you may present the scenarios during a subsequent class period.

SCENARIO SUGGESTIONS:

1. Choose one or more scenarios. Read each chosen scenario to the students. Allow time for discussion after each scenario. Continue the discussion as long as the students offer choices and guidance for Maddie and Alex.

2. Divide the class into groups. Have each group role-play a different scenario illustrating choices based on good character traits. Allow time for discussion after each role-play.

3. Have the students read each scenario. After each scenario has been read, use the following questions to stimulate class discussion.

▸ Introduce the scenarios by saying:

Let's look at the role-plays and see if we can guide Alex and Maddie by using what we know about ways to help our neighbors.

SUGGESTED SCENARIO DISCUSSION QUESTIONS:

Scenario #59

1. *What is the situation or dilemma that Alex is facing?* (Alex is alarmed by the smoke and small explosions coming from his neighbor's house.)

2. *What are Alex's choices?* (Alex can continue watching television. Alex can call 911 and report the problem.)

3. *Have you ever been in a similar situation? Do you feel that you handled the situation with character, displaying citizenship by helping your neighbors?* (Accept all appropriate responses. Keep the students on the topic of being good citizens by helping their neighbors.)

4. *What should Alex choose to say or do?* (Alex must get help. He needs to call 911 and report the problem. Accept all other appropriate responses.)

Scenario #60

1. *What is the dilemma or problem that Alex and Maddie are facing?* (Maddie and Alex have noticed strangers near their neighbors' home and know that their neighbors are not home.)

2. *What are Alex and Maddie's choices?* (Alex and Maddie can just ignore what they saw and "mind their own business." Alex and Maddie can practice good citizenship by getting home and telling their parents or by calling the police themselves.)

3. *Have you ever been in a similar situation? How did you handle it? Was your decision based on good citizenship and helping your neighbors?* (Accept all appropriate responses. Keep the students on the topic of practicing good citizenship by helping our neighbors.)

4. *What should Alex and Maddie choose to say or do?* (Alex and Maddie should quickly let their parents or another adult whom they trust know what is happening at their neighbors' home. They may need to call the police themselves. Accept all other appropriate responses.)

Scenario #61

1. *What is the problem or dilemma that Alex is facing?* (Alex has seen Veronica fall into the deep end of the swimming pool and she seems to not know how to swim.)

2. ***What are Alex's choices?*** (Alex can keep swimming and "mind his own business." Alex can immediately let the lifeguard know about Veronica. If there is no lifeguard, Alex can let an adult know.)

3. ***Have you ever been faced with a similar situation? What did you do? Did you handle the situation based on good citizenship and helping your neighbors?*** (Accept all appropriate responses. Keep the students on the topic of practicing good citizenship by getting involved and helping others.)

4. ***What should Alex choose to say or do?*** (Alex should immediately get help for the child who has fallen into the deep end of the pool. Accept all other appropriate responses.)

Scenario #62

1. ***What is the problem or dilemma that Maddie and Alex are facing?*** (They notice that their neighbor, Mrs. Lopez, is struggling to get her garbage can to the curb for pickup tomorrow.)

2. ***What are Alex and Maddie's choices?*** (Alex and Maddie can ignore Mrs. Lopez and her need for help. They can help her.)

3. ***Have you ever noticed that someone needed help? What did you do? Did you base your decision on good citizenship and helping out in your community?*** (Accept all appropriate responses. Keep the students on the topic of displaying good citizenship by helping their neighbors in their community.)

4. ***What should Alex and Maddie choose to say or do?*** (Alex and Maddie should help Mrs. Lopez. Accept all other appropriate responses.)

Follow-Up Activities:

▸ Revisit the classroom in one week and have the students describe how they have been practicing citizenship by helping their neighbors.

▸ Ask the students to keep a journal for one week and list in it all the various ways they are practicing good citizenship by helping others—either at home, at school, or in the community.

▸ Give each student paper and a pencil. Have the students write original scenarios on the topic of being a good citizen by helping their neighbors.

▸ Revisit the class definition for *citizenship* and check to see if the students feel a need for revisions, additions, or changes.

SCENARIO #59

Alex is home alone watching television. He smells smoke and hears small explosions. Alex looks out the window and sees flames and smoke pouring out of the house next door.

What should Alex choose to say or do?

SCENARIO #60

On the way home from school, Alex and Maddie notice two men hiding in the bushes near their neighbors' window. Alex and Maddie know that the Bassetts are not home from work yet. Alex and Maddie think the men might be trying to break into the Bassetts' home.

What should Alex and Maddie choose to say or do?

SCENARIO #61

Alex and Maddie are swimming with their friends Austen and Stephen at their neighborhood pool. Alex notices that a younger child, Veronica, has fallen into the deep end of the swimming pool. She cannot swim well.

What should Alex choose to say or do?

ALEX & MADDIE: LIFE-SKILL LESSONS THROUGH ROLE-PLAY © 2006 MAR✳CO PRODUCTS, INC. 1-800-448-2197

SCENARIO #62

Alex and Maddie are playing catch when they notice their neighbor, Mrs. Lopez, trying to pull her garbage can to the curb for pickup the next morning. She seems to be struggling to get the can to the curb.

What should Alex and Maddie choose to say or do?

CITIZENSHIP

_____

was caught showing
good character when
displaying _citizenship_ by

_____

_____

_____

Date _____

Signature _____

PERSEVERANCE

Topic Objectives:

To help children realize the value of:

Not giving up.

Continuing to try in the face of defeat.

Seeing a job through to the end.

PERSEVERANCE
INTRODUCTION

Purpose:

To help students understand the meaning of *perseverance*

Materials Needed:

For the leader:
- ☐ Chart paper and marker
- ☐ Masking tape
- ☐ Dictionary (optional)

For each student:
None

Pre-Presentation Preparation:

None

Procedure:

▸ Introduce the topic by having the students define, in their own words, what *perseverance* means to them. Guide the students to a definition.

DEFINITION OF
Perseverance, Persevere

Persevere: to try hard and continuously in spite of obstacles and difficulties

Perseverance: the character trait of being persistent and persevering

> Possible example: A person who perseveres just doesn't give up and keeps on trying.

▸ After the students have agreed on a class definition of *perseverance*, write the definition on chart paper and post the paper in a place in the classroom where everyone can see it for future reference. The students may want to revise or add to the definition as the lessons on perseverance progress. You may give them the definition found above or the dictionary definition. Compare their definition to the formal definition. Make any changes the students or you believe are necessary at this time.

PERSEVERANCE: LESSON 1
"STICK WITH IT" OR "TOUGH IT OUT"

Purpose:

The students will learn that *perseverance* means demonstrating character by sticking with a job or toughing it out to the end. After reading or role-playing the scenarios, the students will apply this knowledge to help Alex and Maddie make decisions requiring perseverance.

Materials Needed:

For the leader:
- ☐ Timer

For each student:
- ☐ Copy of *Scenario #63A* for lower grades (optional, page 183)
- ☐ Copy of *Scenario #63B* for upper grade (optional, page 184)
- ☐ Copy of *Scenario #64* (optional, page 185)
- ☐ Copy of *Scenario #65* (optional, page 186)
- ☐ Copy of *Scenario #66* (optional, page 187)
- ☐ Paper (optional)
- ☐ Pencil (optional)

For each workstation:
- ☐ Paper for collages
- ☐ Markers and/or crayons
- ☐ Scissors
- ☐ Glue
- ☐ Magazines

Pre-Presentation Preparation:

Place paper, glue, markers, crayons, scissors, and magazines at work stations where the students will be working. Decide if you want the students' finished collages posted in the classroom or bound into a book.

Optional: Make a copy of the chosen scenarios for each student or for each student group.

Procedure:

Note: This lesson may be presented during one or more class periods.

▸ Introduce the lesson by asking:

> *Have you ever been in a situation where the task seems to never come to an end, or the work is so hard and boring that it is difficult to keep going and finish the task?* (Accept all appropriate responses.) *If so, you are finding it hard to persevere. It is at times like these that you have the opportunity to display the character trait of* perseverance *and see the job/assignment/task through to the end.*
>
> *You will find paper, glue, markers, crayons, scissors, and magazines at different work stations around the room. I would like each of you to go to a work station and create a collage of situations in which you had to display character by persevering. For example, you might cut out or draw pictures of a person trying to ride a bicycle for the first time or trying to read a sentence for the first time. You will not be in the pictures, but they will illustrate situations that you were faced with at one time or another. When you have finished, write the word* perseverance *at the top of your collage. It's important to put your best effort into this assignment because the collages will be posted in the classroom/bound into our class* Perseverance Book.
>
> *You will have approximately 15 to 20 minutes to complete this assignment.* (Set the timer for 15-20 minutes.)

▸ When the allotted time has elapsed, have the students share their work. Collect all the finished collages. If the students have not finished or would like to elaborate on their collages, have them take the collages home for homework.

▸ If time permits, you may begin the scenarios (pages 183-187) now or you may present the scenarios during a subsequent class period.

▸ Introduce the scenarios by saying:

> *Let's look at the role-plays and see if we can guide Alex and Maddie by using what we know about sticking with a task or toughing it out to the end.*

SCENARIO SUGGESTIONS:

1. Choose one or more scenarios. Read each chosen scenario to the students. Allow time for discussion after each scenario. Continue the discussion as long as the students offer choices and guidance for Maddie and Alex.

2. Divide the class into groups. Have each group role-play a different scenario illustrating choices based on good character traits. Allow time for discussion after each role-play.

3. Have the students read each scenario. After each scenario has been read, use the following questions to stimulate class discussion.

SUGGESTED SCENARIO DISCUSSION QUESTIONS:

Scenario #63A and #63B

1. *What is the problem or dilemma that Alex is facing?* (Alex is frustrated because he has not learned his multiplication tables [sight words for lower grades].)

2. *What are Alex's choices?* (Alex can just quit trying to learn percentages and his times tables [sight words for lower grades]. He can blame the teacher for making the work too hard. Alex can admit that he needs to put more effort into learning his times tables [sight words for lower grades]. He can do more work at home and maybe stay after school for tutoring.)

3. *Have you ever experienced a similar situation? How did you handle it? Did you practice good character by persevering?* (Accept all appropriate responses. Keep the students on the topic of practicing good character by persevering and not giving up when the task/assignment gets tough.)

4. *What should Alex choose to say or do?* (Alex should not give up. He should find ways to get extra help—parents, flash cards, tutoring, etc. Accept all other appropriate responses.)

Scenario #64

1. *What is the dilemma or problem that Maddie is facing?* (Maddie does not understand her homework and would just like to give up.)

2. *What are Maddie's choices?* (Maddie can just give up. Maddie can keep trying. Maddie can call a friend. Maddie can go into school early tomorrow and ask the teacher for help.)

3. *Have you ever not understood your homework or project assignment and just wanted to give up? Did you handle the situation by practicing good character and persevering?* (Accept all appropriate responses. Keep the students on the topic of displaying good character by persevering and seeing a tough job/task through to the end.)

4. *What should Maddie choose to say or do?* (Maddie should not give up. She needs to try to understand the concept with her dad, call a friend, or go into school early tomorrow and ask the teacher for help. Accept all other appropriate responses.)

Scenario #65

1. *What is the situation or problem that Alex is facing?* (Alex's soccer team is losing and there is very little time left to make a comeback.)

2. *What are Alex's choices?* (Alex can give up like his teammates. Alex can show some character by trying to encourage his teammates not to give up.)

3. *Have you ever been in a similar situation? How did you handle it? Do you feel that you handled the situation by displaying character and perseverance?* (Accept all appropriate responses. Keep the students on the topic of showing good character by persevering and not giving up when the going gets tough.)

4. *What should Alex choose to say or do?* (Alex should not give up. He should try to encourage his teammates to play to the best of their ability. Accept all other appropriate responses.)

Scenario #66

1. *What is the problem or dilemma that Maddie is facing?* (Maddie is very frustrated with her lack of success at trying out for the basketball team.)

2. *What are Maddie's choices?* (Maddie can give up and quit even before the coach has selected a team. Maddie can practice and try harder.)

3. *Have you ever tried out for a team and felt frustrated when you didn't do things quite right? Did you handle the situation by displaying character and perseverance?* (Accept all appropriate responses. Keep the students on the topic of displaying good character by persevering and not giving up.)

4. *What should Maddie choose to say or do?* (Maddie should keep trying and should not give up. Accept all other appropriate responses.)

Follow-Up Activities:

▸ Bind the finished collages into your class *Perseverance Book* or post them throughout the classroom.

▸ Give each student paper and a pencil. Have the students write original scenarios focusing on the character trait of perseverance.

SCENARIO #63A

Mrs. Peyton, Alex's teacher, is teaching the class how to read. Alex is struggling because he hasn't learned his sight words. He just wants to give up.

What should Alex choose to say or do?

SCENARIO #63B

Mrs. Peyton, Alex's teacher, is teaching the class how to divide into percentages. Alex is struggling because he hasn't memorized his multiplication tables. He just wants to give up.

What should Alex choose to say or do?

 ALEX & MADDIE: LIFE-SKILL LESSONS THROUGH ROLE-PLAY © 2006 MAR✳CO PRODUCTS, INC. 1-800-448-2197

SCENARIO #64

Maddie has homework tonight that she does not understand. She asks her dad for help, but she still does not understand. She is frustrated and just wants to give up.

What should Maddie choose to say or do?

SCENARIO #65

Alex is playing soccer after school and on weekends for a league team. Today his team is losing 6 to 3 with 10 minutes left in the game. The other boys on Alex's team are getting frustrated and starting to give up.

What should Alex choose to say or do?

 ALEX & MADDIE: LIFE-SKILL LESSONS THROUGH ROLE-PLAY © 2006 MAR*CO PRODUCTS, INC. 1-800-448-2197

SCENARIO #66

Maddie is trying out for an after-school basketball team. At the first afternoon tryout, Maddie does okay. At the second afternoon tryout, Maddie does everything wrong. She is very discouraged and disappointed with herself. She wants to quit trying out for the team.

What should Maddie choose to say or do?

PERSEVERANCE: LESSON 2
THUMBS UP/THUMBS DOWN

Purpose:

The students will recognize perseverance in short examples of student attitude and will signify *perseverance* by putting their thumbs up or signify *no perseverance* by putting their thumbs down. After reading or role-playing the scenarios, the students will guide Alex and Maddie in decisions requiring perseverance.

Materials Needed:

For the leader:
- ☐ Copy of *Thumbs-Up/Thumbs-Down* (page 192)

For each student:
- ☐ Copy of *Scenario #67A* for lower-grade students (optional, page 193)
- ☐ Copy of *Scenario #67B* for upper-grade students (optional, page 194)
- ☐ Copy of *Scenario #68* (optional, page 195)
- ☐ Copy of *Scenario #69* (optional, page 196)
- ☐ Copy of *Scenario #70* (optional, page 197)
- ☐ Paper (optional)
- ☐ Pencil (optional)

Pre-Presentation Preparation:

Make a copy of *Thumbs-Up/Thumbs-Down* for the leader.

Optional: Make a copy of the chosen scenarios for each student or for each student group.

Procedure:

Note: This lesson may be presented during one or more class periods.

▸ Instruct the students to show a "thumbs-up" sign if they believe the student in the example is demonstrating good character by displaying perseverance. Instruct the students to show a "thumbs-down" sign if they believe the student in the example is *not* demonstrating good character by displaying perseverance. Discuss any discrepancies in "thumbs-up" or "thumbs-down" with the students as you read each example.

ALEX & MADDIE: LIFE-SKILL LESSONS THROUGH ROLE-PLAY © 2006 MAR✶CO PRODUCTS, INC. 1-800-448-2197

‣ Read *Thumbs-Up/Thumbs-Down,* citing examples of students' attitudes and displays of perseverance or lack thereof.

‣ If time permits, you may begin the scenarios (pages 193-197) now or you may present the scenarios during a subsequent class period.

‣ Introduce the scenarios by saying:

> ***Let's look at the role-plays and see if we can guide Alex and Maddie by using what we know about perseverance.***

SCENARIO SUGGESTIONS:

1. Choose one or more scenarios. Read each chosen scenario to the students. Allow time for discussion after each scenario. Continue the discussion as long as the students offer choices and guidance for Maddie and Alex.

2. Divide the class into groups. Have each group role-play a different scenario illustrating choices based on good character traits. Allow time for discussion after each role-play.

3. Have the students read each scenario. After each scenario has been read, use the following questions to stimulate class discussion.

SUGGESTED SCENARIO DISCUSSION QUESTIONS:

Scenario #67A and 67B

1. ***What is the dilemma or situation that Maddie is facing?*** (Maddie is getting frustrated as she tries to learn her sight words [long division for upper grades].)

2. ***What are Maddie's choices?*** (Maddie can try harder and ask for extra help at school and at home. Maddie can stop trying.)

3. ***Have you ever felt frustrated because you didn't learn a new concept as quickly as you would have liked? Did you handle the situation with character by displaying perseverance?*** (Accept all appropriate responses. Keep the students on the topic of showing good character by persevering and not giving up.)

4. ***What should Maddie choose to say or do?*** (Maddie should definitely keep trying and should not give up. She should ask for extra help at school and at home. Accept all other appropriate responses.)

Scenario #68

1. *What is the dilemma or problem that Alex is facing?* (Alex is frustrated and nervous about his performance today at spelling bee practice.)

2. *What are Alex's choices?* (Alex can continue to practice and try to do his very best. Alex can just give up.)

3. *Have you ever been in a similar situation? How did you handle it? Did you handle the situation with character by showing perseverance?* (Accept all appropriate responses. Keep the students on the topic of displaying good character by persevering, continuing to try, and not giving up.)

4. *What should Alex choose to say or do?* (Alex should continue to practice for the spelling bee and just do the very best he can to represent his class. Accept all other appropriate responses.)

Scenario #69

1. *What is the situation or problem that Maddie is facing?* (Maddie is frustrated because she is having trouble learning to shoot a basketball.)

2. *What are Maddie's choices?* (Maddie can continue to try and persevere. She can practice at home, after school, and on the weekends. Maddie can just give up and refuse to try.)

3. *Have you ever been in a similar situation? How did you handle your frustration? Did you handle the situation with character by displaying perseverance?* (Accept all appropriate responses. Keep the students on the topic of displaying good character by continuing to persevere and try.)

4. *What should Maddie choose to say or do?* (Maddie should continue to try to learn how to shoot a basketball. She needs to practice often. Accept all other appropriate responses.)

Scenario #70

1. *What is the problem or dilemma that Alex is facing?* (Alex is frustrated as he learns how to skateboard.)

2. *What are Alex's choices?* (Alex can continue to persevere and try to learn how to skateboard. He can practice more. Alex can just give up.)

3. *Have you ever been in a similar situation? How did you handle your frustration? Did you show character by persevering?* (Accept all appropriate responses. Keep the students on the topic of demonstrating good character by continuing to try and persevere.)

4. *What should Alex choose to say or do?* (Alex should continue to try to learn how to skateboard. He needs to practice and persevere. Accept all other appropriate responses.)

Follow-Up Activities:

▸ Have the students keep a journal for a day/week (leader decides length of time) and record instances in which they persevered when they could have just given up. At the end of the determined time, ask the students to elaborate on why they felt successful or unsuccessful in each instance.

▸ Students can make their own lists for a *Thumbs-Up/Thumbs-Down* exercise.

▸ Give each student paper and a pencil. Have the students write original scenarios on the topic of practicing good character by persevering.

▸ Revisit the class definition for *perseverance* and check to see if the students feel a need for revisions, additions, or changes.

THUMBS-UP/THUMBS-DOWN

1. I have a learning disability, so it is okay if I make excuses for myself and give up. *(Thumbs-Down)*

2. I have a big spelling test on Friday. I have studied a little bit every night in the hope that I'll get a good grade. *(Thumbs-Up)*

3. Coach has been teaching us to throw a ball at a target from a certain distance. I am having trouble reaching the target. I go home every night and practice with my dad. I am getting better each day. *(Thumbs-Up)*

4. I am left-handed and my teacher is always asking me to write more legibly. I simply can't! I am left-handed. *(Thumbs-Down)*

5. Our class is planting a garden. Each of us has a spot to take care of. The weeds are growing, and I hate pulling weeds. My area is full of weeds! I give up. *(Thumbs-Down)*

6. I have missed four days of school. I am behind in all my work and it seems like I will never make up all the work I have missed. I am trying very hard to complete my work and turn in all my assignments. I will get it finished! *(Thumbs-Up)*

7. Our school is having a canned-food drive. There is a prize for the class that brings in the most cans. I keep forgetting to bring my canned food from home. It's okay because the other kids in my class will bring in enough. *(Thumbs-Down)*

8. On my last visit, the dentist told me I had my first cavity. I brush every night in the hope that I won't get another cavity in my teeth. *(Thumbs-Up)*

SCENARIO #67A

Maddie is learning sight words so that she can begin reading. Her teacher has sent home sight-word cards that Maddie's parents can help her with at home. Maddie does not want to review the cards after dinner and is considering making up excuses not to study them at home.

What should Maddie choose to say or do?

SCENARIO #67B

Maddie is learning long division. Her teacher has sent home long division flash cards that Maddie's parents can help her with at home. Maddie does not want to review the flash cards after dinner and is considering making up excuses not to study them at home.

What should Maddie choose to say or do?

 ALEX & MADDIE: LIFE-SKILL LESSONS THROUGH ROLE-PLAY © 2006 MAR*CO PRODUCTS, INC. 1-800-448-2197

SCENARIO #68

Alex is representing his class in the school spelling bee. He has studied very hard at home. At practice today, he got nervous and missed all the words he was asked to spell. He goes home and tells his parents he wants to quit.

What should Alex choose to say or do?

SCENARIO #69

Coach Vargas is showing the students in Maddie's class how to shoot a basketball. Maddie always seems to miss the basket. She wants to give up. She is thinking about making an excuse and not going to physical education class tomorrow.

What should Maddie choose to say or do?

 ALEX & MADDIE: LIFE-SKILL LESSONS THROUGH ROLE-PLAY © 2006 MAR*CO PRODUCTS, INC. 1-800-448-2197

SCENARIO #70

Alex got a skateboard for his birthday. He keeps falling off of it. He is ready to just quit trying to learn how to skateboard.

What should Alex choose to say or do?

PERSEVERANCE

_____

was caught showing
good character when
displaying _perseverance_ by

_____

_____

_____

Date _____

Signature _____

ALEX & MADDIE: LIFE-SKILL LESSONS THROUGH ROLE-PLAY © 2006 MAR*CO PRODUCTS, INC. 1-800-448-2197

VOLUNTEERISM

Topic Objectives:

To help children realize the value of:

Offering to help others without expecting anything in return.

Performing a service at home, at school,
or in the community for no reason other than you would like to do it.

Volunteering your talents/time.

VOLUNTEERISM
INTRODUCTION

Purpose:

To help students understand the meaning of *volunteerism*

Materials Needed:

For the leader:
☐ Chart paper and marker
☐ Masking tape
☐ Dictionary (optional)

For each student:
None

Pre-Presentation Preparation:

None

Procedure:

▸ Introduce the topic by having the students define, in their own words, what *volunteerism* means to them. Guide the students to a definition.

> Possible example: A person who offers to help someone or some organization/club without expecting anything in return.

▸ After the students have agreed on a class definition of *volunteerism*, write the definition on chart paper and post the paper in a place in the classroom where everyone can see it for future reference. The students may want to revise or add to the definition as the lessons on volunteerism progress. You may give them the definition found above or the dictionary definition. Compare their definition to the formal definition. Make any changes the students or you believe are necessary at this time.

DEFINITION OF
Volunteer, Volunteerism

Volunteer: a person who undertakes a task or service of his or her own free will

Volunteerism: the habit of volunteering

VOLUNTEERISM: LESSON 1
WHO VOLUNTEERS?

Purpose:

The students will identify volunteer positions in the community and find a volunteer opportunity for themselves. After reading or role-playing the scenarios, the students will apply their knowledge of showing good character by volunteering to help guide Alex and Maddie in their decisions.

Materials Needed:

For the leader:
- ☐ Chalkboard and chalk
- ☐ Timer
- ☐ Copies of *Citizenship And Volunteerism Award* (optional, page 206)

For each student:
- ☐ Newspapers and markers for upper grades
- ☐ Drawing paper and crayons for lower grades
- ☐ Copy of *Scenario #71* (optional, page 207)
- ☐ Copy of *Scenario #72* (optional, page 208)
- ☐ Copy of *Scenario #73* (optional, page 209)
- ☐ Copy of *Scenario #74* (optional, page 210)
- ☐ Paper (optional)
- ☐ Pencil (optional)

Pre-Presentation Preparation:

If you choose to give out awards, make copies of the *Citizenship And Volunteerism Award.* Prior to giving the award, fill in the blanks and circle the act of citizenship that was performed.

Optional: Make a copy of the chosen scenarios for each student or for each student group.

Procedure:

Note: This lesson may be presented during one or more class periods.

▸ Introduce the lesson by saying:

> *Boys and girls, there are jobs at home, in school, and in this city for which no money is paid. The people who do these jobs are called* volunteers. *They volunteer their time and/or talent for the common good. In our classroom, for example, we have Room Mothers and Fathers. They help us with our class parties, field trips, and much more. The school does not pay these people, but things run more smoothly because of their willingness to help. Volunteer jobs are very important to our school community.*
>
> *Can you give me other examples of people who volunteer their time in the classroom or school, church, clubs, after-school teams, or community? Remember: These are jobs for which the person receives no money.*

▸ List the students' examples on the chalkboard.

▸ Distribute the newspapers and markers to the older students and ask them circle with markers stories that cite examples of those who help/volunteer in your community. Remind them that these are non-paying jobs. (This activity can be done individually or in small groups of two or three students.)

For the younger students, distribute drawing paper and crayons. Ask them to draw three examples of people volunteering at school or in the community. Remind the students that they are drawing jobs for which the person is not paid any money.

• After 10-20 minutes, depending on the class, collect the drawings or reports. The students will share them at the next lesson. Then say:

> *Imagine how things would be if there were no volunteers. These jobs would not get done. Volunteers make the community a better place. We would not be able to get along without volunteers. Although we have been talking about adults, even students your age have a responsibility to make the community a better place. Can you think of any needs in our school or community which you could volunteer to meet?* (Accept all appropriate responses.) *Please keep in mind the one job you would like to volunteer to do.*

▸ If time permits, you may begin the scenarios (pages 207-210) now or you may present the scenarios during a subsequent class period.

▸ Introduce the scenarios by saying:

> *Let's look at the role-plays and see if we can guide Alex and Maddie by using what we know about being a volunteer.*

SCENARIO SUGGESTIONS:

1. Choose one or more scenarios. Read each chosen scenario to the students. Allow time for discussion after each scenario. Continue the discussion as long as the students offer choices and guidance for Maddie and Alex.

2. Divide the class into groups. Have each group role-play a different scenario illustrating choices based on good character traits. Allow time for discussion after each role-play.

3. Have the students read each scenario. After each scenario has been read, use the following questions to stimulate class discussion.

SUGGESTED SCENARIO DISCUSSION QUESTIONS:

Scenario #71

1. *What is the dilemma or problem that Alex is facing?* (Alex's classmates are being negative about the idea of volunteering for Pride Day. Alex is confused.)

2. *What are Alex's choices?* (Alex can go along with the other students, complain, and not be a part of Pride Day. Alex can show good character by volunteering to help at Pride Day and not worry about what the other students say or think.)

3. *Have you ever been in a similar situation? How did you handle it? Did your decision show good character by volunteering your time and energy?* (Accept all appropriate responses. Keep the students on the topic of displaying good character by volunteering.)

4. *What should Alex choose to say or do? (*Alex should do what is right and volunteer for Pride Day. Of course, Alex should make sure that he has a parent's permission to participate. Accept all other appropriate responses.)

Scenario #72

1. *What is the dilemma or problem that Maddie is facing?* (Julia and Marta are making fun of those who volunteer to read to the younger students. Maddie is hesitant to volunteer.)

2. *What are Maddie's choices?* (Maddie can volunteer to read to the younger students and not worry about what Julia and Marta might say. Maddie can ignore Mrs. Peyton's request for volunteers and give in to the peer pressure from Julia and Marta.)

3. *Have you ever faced a similar situation? What did you do? Did you show good character by volunteering?* (Accept all appropriate responses. Keep the students on the topic of showing good character by volunteering in their communities.)

4. *What should Maddie choose to say or do?* (Maddie should volunteer to read to the younger students and ignore whatever Julia and Marta say. Accept all other appropriate responses.)

Scenario #73

1. *What is the situation or dilemma that Alex is facing?* (Alex has to decide whether to mow the lawn or play basketball.)

2. *What are Alex's choices?* (Alex can tell his friends that he can't make the game and volunteer to mow the lawn by himself. Alex can play basketball and not mow the lawn. Alex can talk with his father about mowing the lawn on another day.)

3. *Have you ever been in a similar situation? How did you handle it? Do you feel that you handled it with good character by volunteering?* (Accept all appropriate responses. Keep the students on the topic of showing good character by volunteering in all communities—home, school, neighborhood, city, nation, etc.)

4. *What should Alex choose to say or do?* (Alex should volunteer to mow the lawn on Saturday or another day. Accept all other appropriate responses.)

Scenario #74

1. *What is the problem or dilemma that Alex is facing?* (Alex is considering volunteering to keep score for Coach Vargas, even though it is not the "cool" thing to do.)

2. *What are Alex's choices?* (Alex can volunteer to keep score for Coach Vargas during the basketball game. Alex can just ignore Coach Vargas' request for volunteers.)

3. *Have you ever wanted to volunteer for something that others did not think was the "cool" thing to do? What did you end up doing? Was your choice based on good character and volunteering?* (Accept all appropriate responses. Keep the students on the topic of showing good character by volunteering in their communities.)

4. *What should Alex choose to say or do?* (Alex should definitely volunteer to help Coach Vargas keep score during the basketball game this Saturday and ignore the negative peer pressure. He should make sure that he has his parents' permission to do so. Accept all other appropriate responses.)

Follow-Up Activities:

▸ Ask students to keep a journal for a week (or other length of time) listing all the different ways in which they volunteered. At the end of the determined time, ask the students how they felt after they had done the volunteer work/task.

▸ Give each student paper and a pencil. Have the students write original scenarios focusing on showing good character by volunteering their time and/or talents.

▸ Show the students the *Citizenship And Volunteerism Award.* Explain that volunteerism is closely related to good citizenship. Review the four actions listed at the bottom of the award. Then explain how each action relates to good citizenship and volunteerism. For example: If you volunteer to clean up a local park, you are being a good citizen by helping to keep your neighborhood clean. Tell the students you will be watching them and, every time one of them volunteers to do something that shows good citizenship, he/she may win an award. A student who volunteers to do something that shows good citizenship away from school should inform you of the act and when and where it took place.

CITIZENSHIP AND VOLUNTEERISM AWARD

_____

SHOWED GOOD
CITIZENSHIP AND VOLUNTEERISM
WHEN SEEN

Cooperating

Making his/her family, school, and community a better place

Taking care of the environment

Helping a neighbor

DATE _____ LEADER _____

 ALEX & MADDIE: LIFE-SKILL LESSONS THROUGH ROLE-PLAY © 2006 MAR*CO PRODUCTS, INC. 1-800-448-2197

SCENARIO #71

Alex's school is celebrating Pride Day this Saturday with a school wide cleanup from 9-12. Students are asked to sign up to volunteer. The boys in Alex's class are complaining about having to help. They feel that they should get paid or get some sort of extra credit for the work.

What should Alex choose to say or do?

SCENARIO #72

Maddie's teacher, Mrs. Peyton, has asked the students in the class to volunteer to read to younger students in the library during their lunchtime. Julia and Marta are making fun of anyone who volunteers.

What should Maddie choose to say or do?

 ALEX & MADDIE: LIFE-SKILL LESSONS THROUGH ROLE-PLAY © 2006 MAR*CO PRODUCTS, INC. 1-800-448-2197

SCENARIO #73

Alex helps his dad mow the lawn every Saturday. He has never used the lawnmower by himself, but knows he could. Alex just found out that his dad has to go on a business trip this weekend. Alex already promised his friends that he would play basketball with them after he finishes mowing the lawn. Without Dad's help, it will take twice as long to mow the lawn. By the time he finishes, the game will be over.

What should Alex choose to say or do?

SCENARIO #74

Coach Vargas has asked for volunteers to keep score at the basketball game this Saturday. No one wants to volunteer because you don't get paid, you have to give up your Saturday morning, and it just isn't a "cool" thing to do. Alex is thinking about volunteering to keep score.

What should Alex choose to say or do?

 ALEX & MADDIE: LIFE-SKILL LESSONS THROUGH ROLE-PLAY © 2006 MAR*CO PRODUCTS, INC. 1-800-448-2197

VOLUNTEERISM: LESSON 2
HOW CAN I HELP?

Purpose:

The students will determine needs in their school, homes, neighborhoods, and city, and choose their own way to serve as volunteers. After reading or role-playing the scenarios, the students will apply their knowledge of community needs for volunteerism and help guide Alex and Maddie in their decisions.

Materials Needed:

For the leader:
- ☐ Students' drawings or reports from Lesson 1
- ☐ Chalkboard and chalk or chart paper and marker
- ☐ Supplies for binding the *How I Can Help* book

For each student:
- ☐ Copy of *Scenario #75* (optional, page 215)
- ☐ Copy of *Scenario #76* (optional, page 216)
- ☐ Copy of *Scenario #77* (optional, page 217)
- ☐ Copy of *Scenario #78* (optional, page 218)
- ☐ Paper for the *How I Can Help* book
- ☐ Paper (optional)
- ☐ Pencil (optional)

Pre-Presentation Preparation:

Optional: Make a copy of the chosen scenarios for each student or for each student group.

Procedure:

Note: This lesson may be presented during one or more class periods.

▸ Distribute the students' drawings/reports from Lesson 1. Then introduce the lesson by saying:

> ***In our previous lesson, we focused on the people who volunteer in our communities and how important and valuable their volunteerism is for the good of the entire community.***

▸ Have the students share their drawings/reports with the class. Then say:

Now let's focus on how you can help with the various needs and tasks that we find in our school, homes, neighborhoods, and communities. As you think of ways you can volunteer, I'll write them on the chalkboard/chart paper.

▸ Write the students' suggestions on the chalkboard/chart paper.

Possible responses: (Talk about the tasks/needs that people appreciate help with—carrying something heavy, shoveling snow, sweeping cut grass, pulling weeds, cleaning up, help with a school assignment/homework, etc.)

▸ Then say:

We have made a list of possible tasks or jobs for which volunteers might be needed in our communities. As you look at this list, please choose one task or community need that you think you could volunteer to do or fill. Remember: You must first make sure that your parents give you permission to volunteer. Once you have permission for your personal volunteer choice, please commit to this task for one week (or whatever length of time the leader decides is best).

The next time we meet, you must report to the class about your volunteer experience. Your report should include a paragraph about your experience and an illustration to go with it. (For lower grades, the report will consist of illustrations and two or three sentences dictated to the teacher or a parent, who will write the sentences on the paper.) *I will provide the paper for this assignment, because we will bind the finished reports into our class* How I Can Help Book.)

▸ Give each student paper for the *How I Can Help* book. Tell the students to bring their completed reports to the next lesson on (<u>DATE AND TIME OF THE NEXT MEETING</u>). Be sure to stress that students must have parental permission before volunteering.

▸ If time permits, you may begin the scenarios (pages 215-218) now or you may present the scenarios during a subsequent class period.

▸ Introduce the scenarios by saying:

Let's look at the role-plays and see if we can guide Alex and Maddie by using what we know about ways students can volunteer.

SCENARIO SUGGESTIONS:

1. Choose one or more scenarios. Read each chosen scenario to the students. Allow time for discussion after each scenario. Continue the discussion as long as the students offer choices and guidance for Maddie and Alex.

2. Divide the class into groups. Have each group role-play a different scenario illustrating choices based on good character traits. Allow time for discussion after each role-play.

3. Have the students read each scenario. After each scenario has been read, use the following questions to stimulate class discussion.

SUGGESTED SCENARIO DISCUSSION QUESTIONS:

Scenario #75

1. *What is the dilemma or problem that Alex is facing?* (Alex wants to volunteer to visit the retirement home but is confused by peer pressure.)

2. *What are Alex's choices?* (Alex can ignore the request for volunteers and just forget about visiting the retirement home. Alex can volunteer to visit the retirement home after he has asked permission from his parents.)

3. *Have you ever faced a similar situation? How did you handle it? Was your decision based on good character and volunteerism?* (Accept all appropriate responses. Keep the students on the topic of showing good character by volunteering in their communities.)

4. *What should Alex choose to say or do?* (Once Alex has discussed visiting the retirement home with his parents and has their permission, he should volunteer to go. Accept all other appropriate responses.)

Scenario #76

1. *What is the dilemma or problem that Alex and Maddie are facing?* (Both Alex and Maddie would like to be involved in the Walk-a-Thon for charity, but don't know how to get involved.)

2. *What are Alex and Maddie's choices?* (Alex and Maddie can just forget about the Walk-a-Thon and not ask questions about how to volunteer. Alex and Maddie can ask their parents for help on how to become involved in the Walk-a-Thon.)

3. *Have you ever faced a similar situation? How did you handle it? Was your decision based on good character and volunteerism?* (Accept all appropriate responses. Keep the students on the topic of showing good character by volunteering in their communities.)

4. *What should Alex and Maddie choose to say or do?* (Alex and Maddie should ask their parents for permission to participate in the Walk-a-Thon and ask them to help them investigate how to become involved. Accept all other appropriate responses.)

Scenario #77

1. *What is the situation that Alex and Maddie are facing?* (Alex and Maddie know that Mrs. Fonseca will have difficulty getting around with the three inches of snow on her sidewalk and driveway.)

2. **What are Alex and Maddie's choices?** (Alex and Maddie can do absolutely nothing and just forget about Mrs. Fonseca. Alex and Maddie can talk with their parents and figure out how best to help Mrs. Fonseca.)

3. **Have you ever been in a situation where you could volunteer to help a neighbor? Did you show good character by volunteering?** (Accept all appropriate responses. Keep the students on the topic of showing good character by volunteering in their communities.)

4. **What should Alex and Maddie choose to say or do?** (Alex and Maddie should speak with their parents and get their permission to help Mrs. Fonseca. They can brainstorm ideas on how to help her. Accept all other appropriate responses.)

Scenario #78

1. **What is the situation that Alex and Maddie are facing?** (Alex and Maddie would like to see if their neighbors would like to help in the Hurricane Relief Drive at school.)

2. **What are Alex and Maddie's choices?** (Alex and Maddie have already donated to the Hurricane Relief Drive at school, so they could just forget about doing anything more. Alex and Maddie can get permission from their parents to ask some of their neighbors for donations.)

3. **Have you ever been in a similar situation? How did you handle it? Did you handle it by showing good character and volunteering?** (Accept all appropriate responses. Keep the students on the topic of showing good character by volunteering in their communities.)

4. **What should Alex and Maddie choose to say or do?** (Alex and Maddie should first get permission from their parents to ask some of their neighbors if they are interested in donating items to the Hurricane Relief Drive at their school. Accept all other appropriate responses.)

Follow-Up Activities:

▸ At the next meeting, have the students share their finished reports (paragraphs and illustrations for the upper grades or drawings and two or three dictated sentences for the lower grades) on their volunteer experience. Collect the finished papers and bind them into a class book entitled *How I Can Help.*

▸ Give each student paper and a pencil. Have the students write original scenarios focusing on the topic of volunteerism.

▸ Revisit the class definition for *volunteerism* and check to see if the students feel a need for revisions, additions, or changes.

SCENARIO #75

On the announcements at school today, Mrs. Schmidt, the school principal, asked for volunteers to visit the retirement home in the community. This will take place in two weeks. Alex is interested. However, some of the students in Alex's classroom are asking why they should bother with the older people.

What should Alex choose to say or do?

SCENARIO #76

While watching television at home, Alex and Maddie see an announcement for a local charity's Walk-a-Thon. The announcement invites all members of the community to come out and help. Alex and Maddie would like to help but don't know how to get more information about participating in the Walk-a-Thon.

What should Alex and Maddie choose to say or do?

 ALEX & MADDIE: LIFE-SKILL LESSONS THROUGH ROLE-PLAY © 2006 MAR*CO PRODUCTS, INC. 1-800-448-2197

SCENARIO #77

Overnight three inches of snow fell in Alex and Maddie's neighborhood. Mrs. Fonseca, their elderly neighbor, will have trouble walking on her sidewalk and driveway. Alex and Maddie always shovel their driveway and sidewalk.

What should Alex and Maddie choose to say or do?

SCENARIO #78

A drive has begun at school for Hurricane Relief. Alex and Maddie have donated items to the cause, but they would really like to do more. Items that are being requested are soap, shampoo, blankets, and toiletries. Alex and Maddie are the only two children in their neighborhood who go to their school. They feel that their neighbors would like to help if they knew about the Hurricane Relief Drive at school.

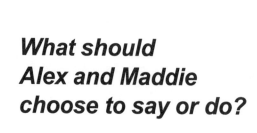

What should Alex and Maddie choose to say or do?

VOLUNTEERISM

_____

was caught showing
good character when
displaying _volunteerism_ by

_____

_____

_____

Date _____

Signature _____

SUPPLEMENTARY ACTIVITY SHEETS

SUPPLEMENTARY ACTIVITY SHEET DIRECTIONS

Alex and Maddie Stick Puppets (Pages 225-226)

Directions: You may choose to have the students make the Alex and Maddie stick puppets as a reminder of the concepts taught in the lessons. Make a copy of the *Alex Stick-Puppet Pattern* and/or *Maddie Stick-Puppet Pattern* for each student. Distribute the activity sheet, a craft/paint stick, glue, scissors, and crayons or markers to each student. You may also make other decorative items, such as yarn and glitter, available. Tell the students to cut out the patterns, then color the puppet and add decorations, such as yarn for hair. Glue each puppet to a paint stick or craft stick.

My Key To Good Character (Page 227)

Directions: Reproduce, on cardstock or heavy-weight paper, a copy of *My Key To Good Character* for each student. Tell the students to hang the key on a door they frequently use as a reminder to practice good character traits. Older students may keep it in their lockers or in their binders.

My Daily Character Thermometer (Pages 228-229)

Directions: Select the *Daily Character Thermometer* appropriate for the age level with which you are working. Make a copy for each student.

Younger students: Distribute an activity sheet and a red crayon to each student. Explain the meaning of the actions on the thermometer and tell the students to fill in their thermometer, starting from the bottom and going up to the kind of day they have had. When everyone has finished, the students may share their thermometers or they may be posted on a bulletin board for the entire class to see. (*Note:* An extension of this activity would be to reproduce the page several times at different intervals and have the students follow the same directions, noting whether their use of character traits has improved.)

Older Students: Distribute the activity sheet and a pencil to each student. Explain that the students are going to keep track of their use of character traits for a period of time you will specify. On the blank lines, have the students write the dates on which they are going to evaluate themselves. Tell them that at the end of the day on each of the dates listed, they are to color their thermometers from the bottom up to the type of day they feel they have had. When all of the dates have passed, have the students share their results with the class.

My Character Promise (Page 230)

Directions: Make a copy of *My Character Promise* and post it in the classroom. Have a student or the entire class recite the promise aloud each day. Copies may be made for each student to keep in his/her binder.

My Daily Character Wallet Checklist (Page 231)

Directions: Reproduce, on cardstock or heavy-weight paper, a copy of *My Daily Character Wallet Checklist* for each student. Distribute the activity sheet and scissors to each student. Have the students cut apart the cards. (*Note:* If possible, laminate the cards. This will help the cards last longer.) Review the information on the cards and instruct the students to carry the cards in their pockets, purses, or wallets.

Variation: A card can be placed on each student's classroom desk as a daily reminder to practice positive behaviors.

My Character Shield (Page 232)

Directions: Make a copy of *My Character Shield* for each student. Distribute the activity sheet and crayons to each student. Have the students write their name on the banner, then color their shield. The students may then take their shields home and post their shields in a prominent spot. Younger students may want to post them on the refrigerator to remind themselves and their parents of the character traits that are being emphasized in class. Older students may wish to keep their shields in their binders.

Character Word Search I and II (Pages 233-234)

Directions: Select the *Character Word Search* appropriate for the age level with which you are working. Make a copy for each student. Distribute the activity sheet and a pencil to each student. Review the directions with the students.

Character Bookmarks (pages 235-236)

Directions: Make enough copies so each student has a bookmark for each character trait. Distribute bookmarks, scissors, and crayons or markers to each student. Have the students color and cut out each bookmark.

The appropriate bookmark can be distributed either before you start a specific lesson or after the lesson is completed.

Variations: Teachers may use the bookmarks as incentives. The bookmarks may be distributed to students who display specific character traits. Encourage the students to earn all eight bookmarks!

The Character Wheel (page 237)

Directions: Reproduce a *Character Wheel* on cardstock or heavy-weight paper for each student. Distribute the activity sheet, scissors, and crayons or markers to each student. Instruct the students to cut out the wheel and the spinner and then decorate their wheel. When everyone has finished, have each student bring his/her *Character Wheel* to you so you can attach the spinner to the center of the wheel with a brad.

Tell the students to spin their spinners. The character trait that the spinner lands on is the one that the student will concentrate on for whatever period of time you specify.

(*Note:* If you do not want to use the spinner, just have the students cut out and decorate the wheel. Then, instead of spinning the spinner, they may close their eyes and point to the character trait they will concentrate on.)

If students are keeping journals, you may wish to have the *Character Wheel* activity at the beginning of the week or day, then have the students record their progress in their journal.

Character Word Scramble I and II (pages 238-239)

Directions: Select the *Character Word Scramble* appropriate for the age level with which you are working. Make a copy for each student. Distribute an activity sheet and a pencil to each student. Review the directions with the students.

The answers to *Character Word Scramble I* are: Trustworthy, Respect, Responsible, Fairness, Caring, Citizenship, Persevere, Volunteer.

The answers to *Character Word Scramble II* are: Care, Caring, Volunteer, Volunteerism, Respect, Respectful, Citizen, Citizenship, Persevere, Perseverance, Trust, Trustworthy, Responsible, Responsibility, Fair, Fairness.

(*Note:* to add a little competition to the assignment, set a timer for a certain amount of time. When the timer goes off, have the students count how many words they have unscrambled. The winner is the student who has unscrambled the most words.)

Secret Code (page 240)

Directions: Make a copy of the activity sheet for each student. Distribute the activity sheet and a pencil to each student. Have the students complete the activity by writing the appropriate letter above each hand sign. When the students have discovered the secret message, discuss its meaning.

The answer is: My Character Is Important.

ALEX STICK-PUPPET PATTERN

MADDIE STICK-PUPPET PATTERN

 ALEX & MADDIE: LIFE-SKILL LESSONS THROUGH ROLE-PLAY © 2006 MAR*CO PRODUCTS, INC. 1-800-448-2197

MY KEY TO GOOD CHARACTER

Reminds me as I go in and out to be:

Trustworthy

Respectful

A Good Citizen

Responsible

Persevering

A Volunteer

Caring

Fair

MY DAILY CHARACTER THERMOMETER

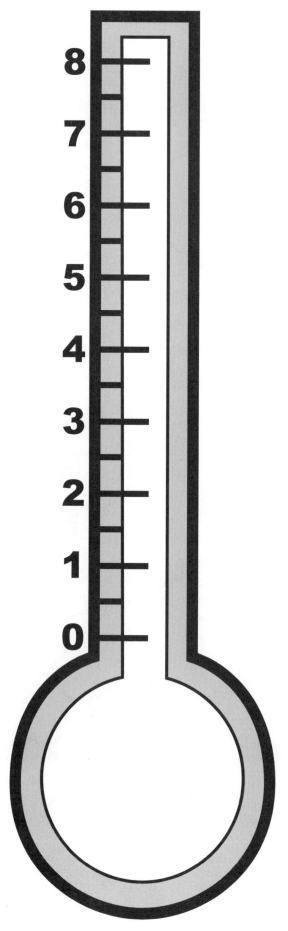

8 AN EXTREMELY GOOD CHARACTER DAY
(I have sincerely worked at being trustworthy, respectful, responsible, fair, caring, a good citizen, persevering, and volunteering.)

7 AN ABOVE-AVERAGE CHARACTER DAY
(I have practiced all but one of the above character traits.)

6 AN AVERAGE CHARACTER DAY
(I have practiced all but two of the above character traits.)

5 MY CHARACTER NEEDS ATTENTION
(I practiced some of the above character traits, and I need to work harder on the others.)

ALEX & MADDIE: LIFE-SKILL LESSONS THROUGH ROLE-PLAY © 2006 MAR*CO PRODUCTS, INC. 1-800-448-2197

MY DAILY CHARACTER THERMOMETER

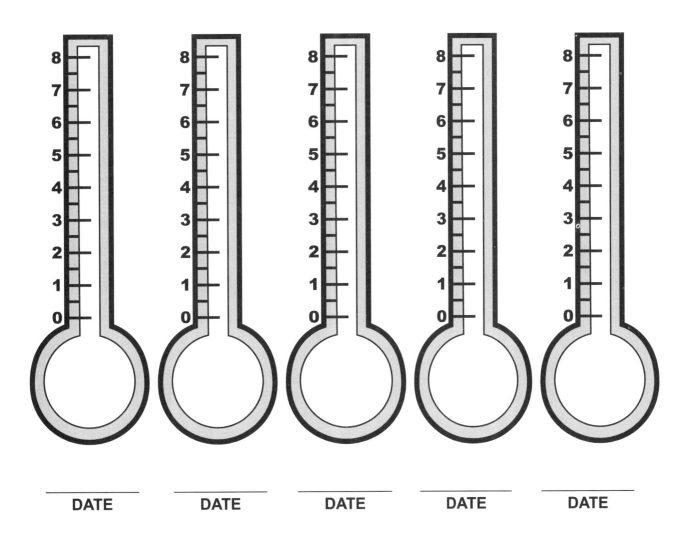

DATE   DATE   DATE   DATE   DATE

8 **AN EXTREMELY GOOD CHARACTER DAY**
(I have sincerely worked at being trustworthy, respectful, responsible, fair, caring, a good citizen, persevering, and volunteering.)

7 **AN ABOVE-AVERAGE CHARACTER DAY**
(I have practiced all but one of the above character traits.)

6 **AN AVERAGE CHARACTER DAY**
(I have practiced all but two of the above character traits.)

5 **MY CHARACTER NEEDS ATTENTION**
(I practiced some of the above character traits, and I need to work harder on the others.)

MY CHARACTER PROMISE

As a member of

_____ ,
NAME OF SCHOOL OR CLASSROOM

I promise to be:

Trustworthy
Respectful
Responsible
Fair
Caring
A Good Citizen
Persevering
A Volunteer

And to always have the courage
to do the right thing.

 MY CHARACTER IS
IMPORTANT TO ME!

MY DAILY CHARACTER WALLET CHECKLIST

I have this card to remind me daily to be trustworthy.

Being *trustworthy* means to:
▸ Tell the truth.
▸ Have loyalty towards family, friends, community, and country.
▸ Be dependable—follow through on what I say I will do.
▸ Not lie, cheat, or steal.

I have this card to remind me daily to be caring.

Being *caring* means to:
▸ Help others in need.
▸ Show kindness and compassion.
▸ Readily forgive others.
▸ Show gratitude to others.

I have this card to remind me daily to be respectful.

Being *respectful* means to:
▸ Do unto others as you would have them do unto you—follow *The Golden Rule*.
▸ Not threaten, yell at, hit, or hurt another person or animal.
▸ Mind my manners and use appropriate language.
▸ Know that it is okay for people to look different, speak different languages, and dress differently.
▸ Act respectfully and peacefully when confronted with anger, bad language, or disagreements.

I have this card to remind me daily to be a good citizen.

Being a good citizen means to:
▸ Obey rules and laws.
▸ Be ready to cooperate.
▸ Show respect for authority.
▸ Do my part to make my family, school, and community a better place and take care of the environment.
▸ Inform myself and vote in school elections.
▸ Help my neighbors.

I have this card to remind me daily to be responsible.

Being *responsible* means to:
▸ Try to always do my very best.
▸ Remember to think before I act—actions have consequences.
▸ Keep trying. Don't give up.
▸ Do what I am supposed to do.
▸ Use self-discipline and self-control.

I have this card to remind me daily to persevere.

To *persevere* means to:
▸ Not give up.
▸ Keep trying in the face of defeat.
▸ See a job through to the end.

I have this card to remind me daily to be fair.

Being *fair* means to:
▸ Share and take turns.
▸ Listen to others and be open-minded.
▸ Follow the rules in everything I do.
▸ Not blame others if things don't work out.
▸ Not to take advantage of others or of their trust.

I have this card to remind me daily to volunteer.

Volunteering means to:
▸ Offer to help others without expecting anything in return.
▸ Perform a service at home, at school, or in the community for no reason other than I would like to.
▸ Volunteer my talents/time.

MY CHARACTER SHIELD

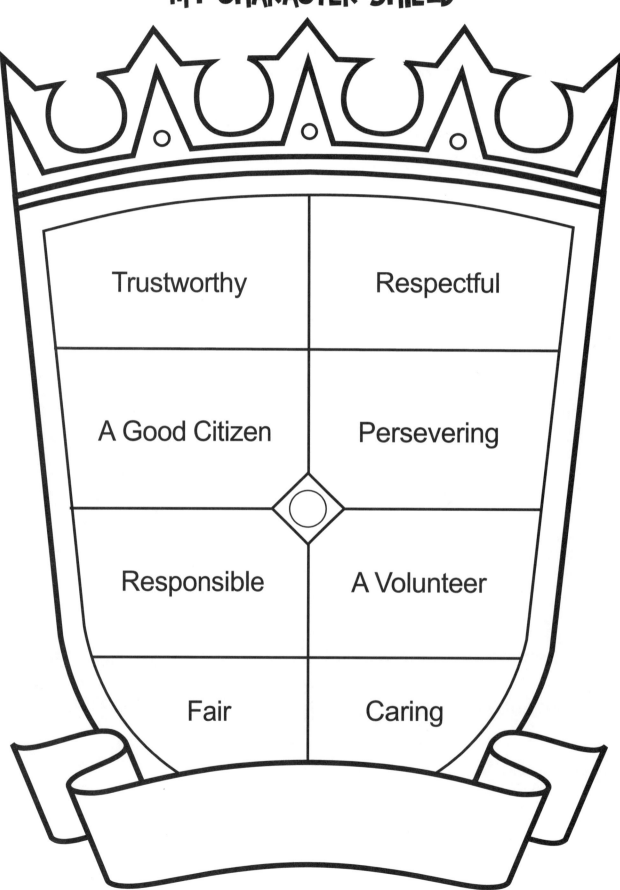

Trustworthy

Respectful

A Good Citizen

Persevering

Responsible

A Volunteer

Fair

Caring

 ALEX & MADDIE: LIFE-SKILL LESSONS THROUGH ROLE-PLAY © 2006 MAR✶CO PRODUCTS, INC. 1-800-448-2197

CHARACTER WORD SEARCH I

Directions: Find the listed words in the word search below. Circle each word when you find it. The words are hidden across, down, and diagonally.

| TRUST | RESPECT | FAIR | RESPONSIBLE |
| CARING | CITIZENSHIP | PERSEVERE | VOLUNTEER |

```
A  P  E  R  S  E  V  E  R  E  O  G
R  T  N  M  V  C  S  C  F  A  I  R
E  V  R  G  H  I  O  I  D  C  Z  E
S  O  V  B  K  T  P  T  I  A  G  S
P  L  B  O  M  I  C  Z  L  U  Y  P
O  U  O  L  U  Z  T  A  E  R  B  E
N  N  R  S  K  E  T  T  R  A  G  C
S  T  V  G  K  N  P  R  I  I  G  T
I  E  V  S  E  S  P  T  U  A  N  S
B  E  V  S  K  H  P  T  I  S  G  G
L  R  V  S  K  I  P  T  I  A  T  S
E  K  S  L  U  P  T  E  E  R  X  P
```

CHARACTER WORD SEARCH II

Directions: Find the listed words in the word search below. Circle each word when you find it. The words are hidden across, down, and diagonally.

RESPECT   RESPONSIBILITY   FAIRNESS   TRUSTWORTHINESS
CARING   CITIZENSHIP   PERSEVERANCE   VOLUNTEERISM
TRUST   RESPECTFUL   RESPONSIBLE   FAIR
CARE   PERSEVERE   VOLUNTEER

```
T R V O L U N T E E R I S M G
N R E J P E R S E V E R E N Y
R R U S V K E A W T D Q I T R
P E F S P W P N V U N R I A E
E S A V T E F C K H A L J X S
R P I W H W C A K C I E V F P
S O R R V S O T I B P F X B E
E N N W R V N R I R Y Q G C C
V S E N A D E S T I U H K J T
E I S L L R N I C H T E J E F
R B S Y A O I Q R L I R U Q U
A L R C P E D V J D B N U V L
N E J S R G K J G H N M E S X
C N E W V O L U N T E E R S T
E R J C I T I Z E N S H I P S
```

ALEX & MADDIE: LIFE-SKILL LESSONS THROUGH ROLE-PLAY © 2006 MAR∗CO PRODUCTS, INC. 1-800-448-2197

CHARACTER BOOKMARKS

TRUSTWORTHY

Tell
the truth.

Be loyal
to family,
friends,
community,
and
country.

Be
dependable.
Follow
through on
what you say
you will do.

Don't lie,
cheat, or steal.

RESPECT

Do unto others
as you would
have them
do unto you.
Follow
The Golden Rule.

Don't threaten,
yell at, hit,
or hurt another
person or animal.

Mind your
manners and use
appropriate
language.

Know that it is
okay for people
to look different,
speak different
languages, and
dress differently.

When confronted
with anger,
bad language, or
disagreements,
handle them
respectfully and
peacefully.

RESPONSIBLE

Try to always
do your
very best.

Remember
to think
before you act.
Actions have
consequences.

Keep trying.
Don't give up.

Do what
you are
supposed to do.

Use
self-discipline
and
self-control.

FAIRNESS

Share and
take turns.

Listen to
others and be
open-minded.

Follow the rules
in everything
you do.

Don't blame
others if things
don't work out.

Be sure not to
take advantage
of others or
of their trust.

CHARACTER BOOKMARKS

PERSEVERANCE

Don't
give up.

Keep trying
in the face
of defeat.

See a job
through
to the end.

CARING

Help others
in need.

Show
kindness
and
compassion.

Readily
forgive
others.

Show
gratitude
to others.

GOOD CITIZENSHIP

Obey rules
and laws.

Be ready
to cooperate.

Show respect
for authority.

Do your part
to make
your family,
school,
and community
a better place
and take
care of the
environment.

Inform
yourself
and vote in
school
elections.

Help your
neighbors.

VOLUNTEERISM

Offer to
help others
without
expecting
anything
in return.

Perform
a service
at home,
at school,
or in the
community
for no reason
other than
you would
like to.

Volunteer
your
talents/time.

 ALEX & MADDIE: LIFE-SKILL LESSONS THROUGH ROLE-PLAY © 2006 MAR*CO PRODUCTS, INC. 1-800-448-2197

CHARACTER WHEEL

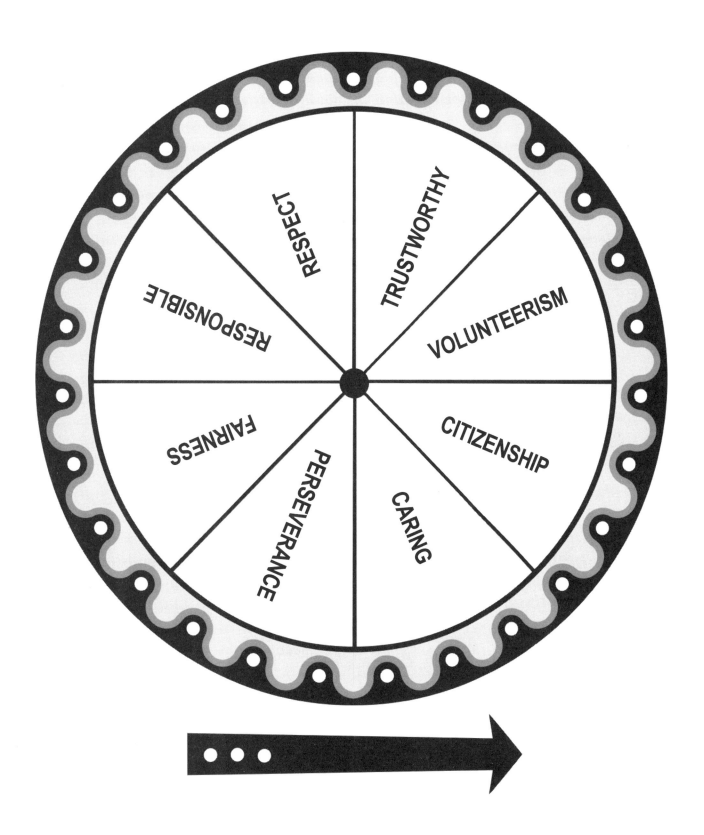

CHARACTER WORD SCRAMBLE I

Directions: Unscramble the following words.

A character trait that means you are honest and people can depend on you.

TOURTTSWRHY   __ __ __ __ __ __ __ __ __ __ __

A character trait that means you treat others as you would like to be treated.

TRPEESC   __ __ __ __ __ __ __

A character trait that means if you are supposed to do something, you do it!

SBERONLEIPS   __ __ __ __ __ __ __ __ __ __ __

A character trait that means you share and take turns.

ESRFIANS   __ __ __ __ __ __ __ __

A character trait that means you help others in need.

GRACNI   __ __ __ __ __ __

A character trait that means you do your part to take care of the environment.

ZPITICESNIH   __ __ __ __ __ __ __ __ __ __ __

A character trait that means you do not give up.

VEEEPRERS   __ __ __ __ __ __ __ __ __

A character trait that means you help others without expecting something in return.

ONLVTRUEE   __ __ __ __ __ __ __ __ __

 ALEX & MADDIE: LIFE-SKILL LESSONS THROUGH ROLE-PLAY © 2006 MAR*CO PRODUCTS, INC. 1-800-448-2197

CHARACTER WORD SCRAMBLE II

Directions: Look at the scrambled words below. Sometimes you will find the same character traits used as a different parts of speech.

ACER   __ __ __ __

GRACNI   __ __ __ __ __ __

ONVLERUTE   __ __ __ __ __ __ __ __ __

TMEEVSUNIORL   __ __ __ __ __ __ __ __ __ __ __ __

TRPEESC   __ __ __ __ __ __ __

FTRPEUESLC   __ __ __ __ __ __ __ __ __ __

ZITNCIE   __ __ __ __ __ __ __

ZPITICESNIH   __ __ __ __ __ __ __ __ __ __ __

VEEEPRERS   __ __ __ __ __ __ __ __ __

CVEAEPNRERSE   __ __ __ __ __ __ __ __ __ __ __ __

URTTS   __ __ __ __ __

YURTWRTTOSH   __ __ __ __ __ __ __ __ __ __ __

SBERONLEIPS   __ __ __ __ __ __ __ __ __ __ __

SYBIRONLTEIPSI   __ __ __ __ __ __ __ __ __ __ __ __ __ __

RIFA   __ __ __ __

NRISFEAS   __ __ __ __ __ __ __ __

SECRET CODE

A B C D E F G

H I J K L M N

O P Q R S T U

V W X Y Z CLAWED HAND . BENT HAND ,

CLAWED HAND

 ALEX & MADDIE: LIFE-SKILL LESSONS THROUGH ROLE-PLAY © 2006 MAR*CO PRODUCTS, INC. 1-800-448-2197